UNDERSTANDING YOUR HORSE'S HEALTH

A PRACTICAL GUIDE

JANET L. ELEY
BVSc. MRCVS

WARD LOCK

First published in Great Britain in 1992
by Ward Lock Limited, Villiers House,
41/47 Strand, London WC2N 5JE, England

A Cassell imprint

British Library Cataloguing in Publication Data
Eley, Janet L.
Understanding your Horse's Health.
I. Title
636.1083

ISBN 0 7063 6963 7

Text filmset in 11/12pt Rockwell
by Columns of Reading Ltd
Printed and bound in Great Britain
by Mackays of Chatham PLC

CONTENTS

ACKNOWLEDGEMENTS

I am most grateful to Jeannette Chapman for typing the manuscript and for her helpful advice in all stages of preparation.

I would like to thank Chris Hocking for taking the photographs and Joan Rogers for her expert handling of the horses and all the owners who kindly allowed their horses to be photographed.

The laminitis photographs were generously provided by Robert Eustace. Thanks also to farriers Barry Oldman, Mark Caldwell and Anne Claxton and to Mustad for providing the photograph of the glue-on shoe. A special thanks to Gill Cooper for all her help.

DEDICATION

To special patients including George, Quest, Capelena, Woofy, Hadleigh, Dougal and Jingles.

SECTION 1
CHOOSING A HEALTHY HORSE

CHAPTER 1
PURCHASING A HORSE

There are a number of important points that you need to consider before purchasing a horse. It will be your responsibility as its owner to provide adequate food, shelter and regular exercise, footcare and grooming. You need to have a knowledge of health care, routine vaccination and worming programmes. And if you do not have the knowledge to care for the animal yourself, it should be kept at a reputable livery yard under expert supervision.

The actual cost of the horse is often well within the prospective purchaser's price range, but unfortunately the day-to-day 'running costs' are frequently overlooked, and it is a fact that most cases of neglect are due to ignorance and lack of money. The tack – saddle, bridle and numnah – plus headcollar, rugs, grooming kit, feed-bowls, hay-nets, etc., also have to be paid for, and once purchased, will require some maintenance.

You will have to pay for stabling, bedding materials, grazing and feed, the price of which may alter throughout the year. Fencing and grassland will also need constant attention to maintain them in good order.

The farrier will be required every 4–6 weeks, and the veterinary surgeon at least twice a year for routine health checks, vaccines and teeth rasping.

It is usual to have an insurance policy to cover accidents and veterinary treatment. These are usually taken out at the time the horse is purchased, and are tailor-made to suit the type of work the animal will be doing and the requirements of the owner. Bear in

CHECKLIST – PRIOR TO PURCHASE

(1) COST

Initial outlay	horse + tack + rugs
Weekly expenses:	rent – field & stables/shelter, bedding, feed ? water rates ? electricity
4–6 weekly expenses:	farrier, worming preparations (anthelmintics)
6 monthly expenses:	veterinary health checks, vaccines, dental care
Yearly expenses:	insurance cover
EXTRAS:	lessons, competition entry fees, transport, clipping, first aid kit
Maintenance costs:	equipment grassland fences & gates stables & shelters
Qualified Groom + **Full Livery**	or **(2)** & **(3)**

(2) TIME

Daily routine:	feeding & watering, grooming, mucking out stable, exercise
Twice weekly:	mucking out field & checking fencing cleaning tack & repairs
Monthly:	farrier, pulling mane & trimming heels & tail
Seasonal:	clipping collecting hay removing poisonous plants from pasture, e.g., ragwort, acorns applying fly repellents
(3) KNOWLEDGE:	stable management & safety feeding & watering foot care & grooming exercise programmes signs of health disease prevention – routine worming, dental care & vaccines when to call the vet first aid & nursing

mind that the cheapest policy is not always the best.

If you can afford both the horse and its upkeep, you must next consider whether you have the time to look after it. There is no point in contemplating buying a horse if you have no time to care for it. It will require attention every day, even when you are ill or on holiday, or just feel like a day off. Anyone who has a hectic lifestyle, with little or no spare time, would be advised to ride at a riding-school or trekking centre, and not to buy a horse.

The type of horse purchased will depend to a great extent on what type of work you want it for, whether hacking or three-day eventing, as an enormous number of horse types and breeds would make suitable hacks, but only a few have the athletic ability to three-day event successfully. It is very important to purchase the right animal – one that can do the job expected of it, and which is within your handling and riding expertise.

The facilities that you have available will also dictate the type of animal that you can keep. For example, a horse which is clipped and rugged up will need stabling and cannot be left out in a field in the middle of winter. A fat, native pony may need to be brought in off the grass in the spring to prevent laminitis (see page 44), whereas a horse with a respiratory hay/straw allergy may need to live out all the year round.

THE SIGNS OF GOOD HEALTH

It is not advisable to purchase an animal in a poor or unhealthy condition. It is therefore important to recognize the signs of good health.

- A healthy horse is bright and alert, taking an interest in its surroundings without being nervous or hyper-active.
- Its coat should lie flat and be glossy. It should be free from bald areas, sores and scabs, and areas of irritation. The skin should be naturally supple and move easily over the underlying fat layer.
- The body condition should be good. The horse preferably should be in regular work and athletically fit so that its temperament can be assessed accurately. A lethargic, fat and unfit horse may become quite lively when slimmed down and

CHECKLIST – THE HORSE'S STATE OF HEALTH

Body condition –	fat > lean
Skin & coat –	glossy, staring, scabs
Behaviour –	nervous, alert > dull
Posture & movement –	abnormal – lame
Appetite & thirst –	good or poor or abnormal
Eyes & nose –	for discharges
Respiration (breathing) –	rate & type, coughing
Temperature –	sweating or cold, i.e., coat standing on end
Pulse –	too fast or slow
Faeces & urine –	normal amount, colour, consistency

fittened. Similarly, a very thin and physically weak animal may not be so quiet and easy to handle when it is at its correct body-weight and in work.

- The eyes and nostrils should be clear of discharges and the breath should smell sweet. Coughing and difficulty in breathing are signs of disease.
- The horse's posture, *i.e.*, the position of its legs, head and neck, is important, as abnormal posture is often a sign of illness and pain, for example, chest pain causes the horse to stand with its elbows away from its rib cage, abdominal pain may cause the horse to stand with an arched back in the urinating position.
- A healthy horse will bear weight on all four legs and should stand square. It will rest a painful limb and its foot may not land flat when bearing weight.
- When moving, the horse's strides ought to be regular in rhythm and length. Stumbling and tripping can be dangerous and are often a sign of navicular syndrome.
- When regularly fed, the horse passes faeces every couple of hours. The amount and texture of the faeces is an indication of its appetite and the availability of food. Normal faeces are soft and formed into balls, and depending on the diet will vary in colour. Grass-fed animals have dark green faecal balls, whereas hay-fed horses have yellowish faeces which break apart quite easily. Horses' urine

can vary in colour from clear to cloudy yellow depending on the amount of crystal deposits. It should not be dark red.

If the horse is being purchased for a novice or inexperienced rider it is vital that it has a nice temperament, good manners and is properly schooled. An experienced person may be able to cope with a horse of dubious temperament, but this would take away some pleasure of ownership. Totally green, uneducated horses are best left to the professional to school.

If you are an inexperienced rider buying your first horse, you should take your instructor or trainer to see it. The instructor will be able to assess if the horse is suitable for you. It is safer to allow the owner to ride the horse before you do, and this will also give you a chance to see problems or difficulties. The type of tack used will also give you an indication of the horse's behaviour when ridden, for example a horse which is suitable for a novice rider can usually be ridden in a snaffle bit.

CHAPTER 2
THE VETERINARY EXAMINATION FOR PURCHASE

It is advisable to have the horse examined by a veterinary surgeon (vet) prior to purchase. Not all vets routinely treat horses, so it is best to choose one who is in equine practice. You should not ask the vendor's vet to examine the horse on your behalf.

You should contact the vet of your choice personally, so that you can discuss any special techniques, such as blood samples and X-rays, that may be needed. The vet will also need to know what sporting activity the horse is being purchased for and to what standard you hope to compete. If you are worried about a particular blemish or health problem, this is the time to mention it. It is always beneficial to be present at the vetting so that any findings can be discussed at that time. It is also of special value as a learning exercise for an inexperienced owner. If you cannot attend the vetting, it is important to describe the horse to be examined carefully so that no mistaken identity can occur!

The standard vetting procedure is divided into five stages and is designed to detect any clinical signs of disease, injury or abnormality that would render the horse unsuitable for purchase for a specific use. This usually takes 1½ to 2 hours depending on the facilities available and how well organized the vendor is.

The horse should be stabled for a couple of hours before examination. The vet will require a riding horse to be exercised, so you must ask the vendor to organize tack and a jockey together with a suitable place to ride. Young and unbroken animals are usually exercised on a lunge rein, so correct lungeing equipment will be required. A hard flat surface such as a driveway or quiet road will also be needed during the examination.

It is preferable that the horse be clean and dry, with the feet picked out but not oiled. If the horse is shod, all four shoes should be in good condition and not hanging off. The vet will also require any documents relating to the horse's age, breeding, height and vaccination history.

STAGE ONE

Stage one of the examination takes place in the stable, where the vet assesses the horse's general condition and conformation. The heart is examined in the resting animal and compared with the heart after strenuous exercise. The body temperature and resting respiratory rate are noted. The eyes are inspected using an ophthalmoscope in the dark box. The teeth are checked to assess the horse's age, and for abnormalities. The vet examines each side of the horse systematically from head to tail. He palpates all the limbs for signs of injury and flexes the joints to detect pain and restricted movement. The feet are checked. If the vet finds no conditions that would prohibit purchase at this stage, the horse is then stood outside.

The vet views the horse from both sides and notes the conformation.

1. Flexing the horse's hind-leg joints to detect pain or restriction in movement.

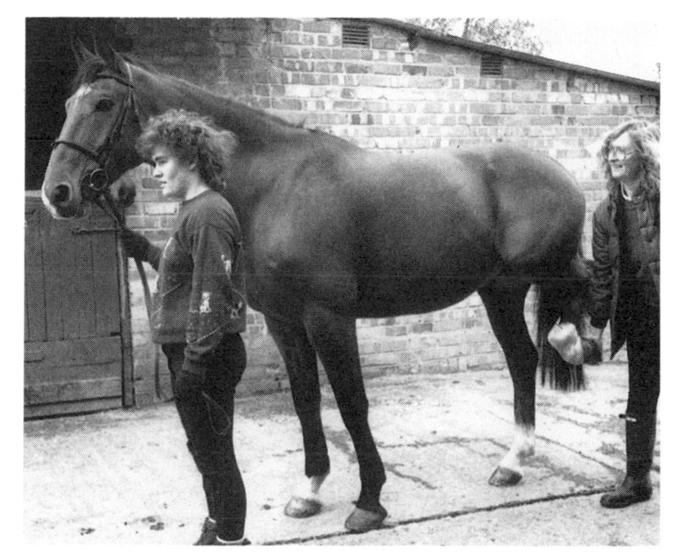

STAGE TWO

Stage two involves walking and trotting the horse away from and towards the vet on a hard level surface. If a public road is being used the horse must be on a bridle. The attendant must not interfere with the horse's way of going or obstruct the vet's view of the horse.

The horse may have abnormal action, or not move straight due to poor conformation of the limbs or injury or disease. If the horse is found to be lame at this stage the examination stops as the lameness may be exacerbated by strenuous exercise. In this case, the vet will advise the purchaser not to buy the horse. Sometimes the owner thinks the condition is of a temporary nature and that the horse will 'come sound'. If this is the case, naturally the animal could be vetted again at a later date. It is the owner's responsibility to call their own vet to examine and treat any conditions found. Your vet is there to examine the horse solely on your behalf.

If no problems have been found so far, the vet may then lunge the horse and do flexion tests on the limbs. Each limb is held up in turn with the joints flexed for a set length of time and then the horse is trotted off. This will show up any pain in the joints, as the horse will trot away lame.

STAGE THREE

Stage three involves exercising the horse either under saddle or on the lunge, depending on its age, size and

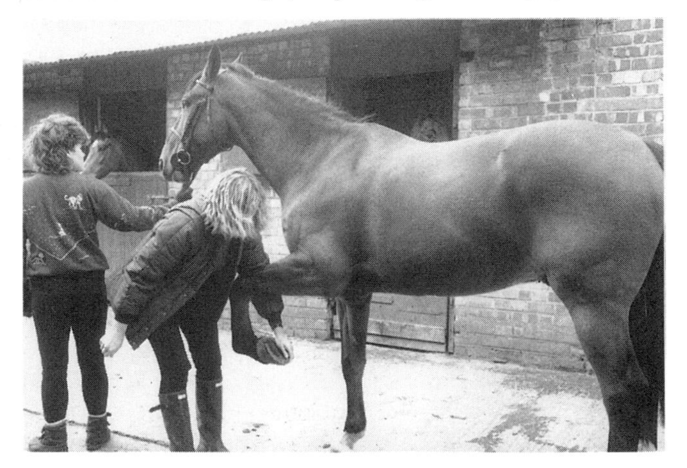

2. Flexing a foreleg to reveal any pain in the joints.

stage of training. Any problems encountered in tacking up or mounting are noted.

It is necessary to give the horse sufficient exercise to make it breathe deeply and rapidly and to increase the heart rate so that any abnormalities can be easily detected. Obviously the amount and type of exercise will depend on the condition and fitness of the animal. It is usual to see the horse ridden at walk, trot and canter on both reins (i.e., in both directions on a circle) and a controlled gallop. The vet reports any signs of napping or naughtiness. He will also look for lameness, especially at the trot and after faster work. He examines the heart and lungs after exercise and during the following rest period (stage four).

STAGE FOUR

The vet fills in the details on the certificate during the rest period. He completes the identification diagrams and written description, and reports any signs of disease or injury observed by this stage of the examination.

STAGE FIVE

When the heart and respiratory rates have returned to the resting rate, the final stage of the examination can proceed. Stage five involves walking and trotting the horse in hand (as in stage two). Often, old sprains and injuries show up after the rest period. The horse is also turned in tight circles to left and right and asked to back up for a few steps. The feet are fully inspected, and if necessary the shoes removed – with the owners permission!

Blood samples may be taken to detect the presence of pain killers or other drugs that the owner may have given the horse prior to the examination to conceal an illness or injury.

The vet lists on the certificate all signs of disease, injury, abnormalities and observations, such as vices, seen during the vetting. The vet then decides whether these findings (if any) will affect the horse's suitability for purchase for the particular work required of it. Some of the findings may be of little consequence and may not affect the performance of the horse, in which case the vet will say that in his/her opinion the horse is suitable for purchase.

Sometimes prospective purchasers ask the vet 'just to give the horse a quick look over' in the hope of saving time and money. This is most unsatisfactory; in fact, it is a waste of time and money. The whole point of vetting is to examine the entire animal thoroughly, so a proper and worthwhile assessment can be made. Most vets refuse to do 'mini vettings'.

WARRANTIES

If it is important to you that the horse will travel in a trailer or is good to catch and shoe, this should be included in a written warranty signed by the vendor. Warranties often cover the horse's height, freedom from vices such as crib biting and rearing, its behaviour in traffic, and proven athletic ability, e.g., show jumping.

SETTLING THE NEW HORSE IN

It may take a little time for you and your new horse to adjust to each other, and there may be a few teething problems. The horse will take less time to settle into its new home if its daily routine is not suddenly changed. Horses are creatures of habit and any changes in management should if possible be gradual.

The horse's diet should not be changed suddenly as this could cause colic. You should find out the type and exact amount of feed (in lbs or kg), including the brands, that the horse is used to. The amount of exercise a horse has affects the amount of food given, so if you are going to alter the horse's work, you must alter its diet accordingly (see page 74). It is very useful to know if the animal has any particular likes or dislikes, or any odd habits or allergies. You will need its worming and vaccination history, and the name of the present farrier and vet. You should make a note of the type and size of its tack if you cannot purchase it with the horse.

Insure the horse before the journey home.

It is best for the horse to arrive at its new home in daylight and on a day when you can spend the whole day with it.

CHAPTER 3
CONFORMATION

Fig. 1.

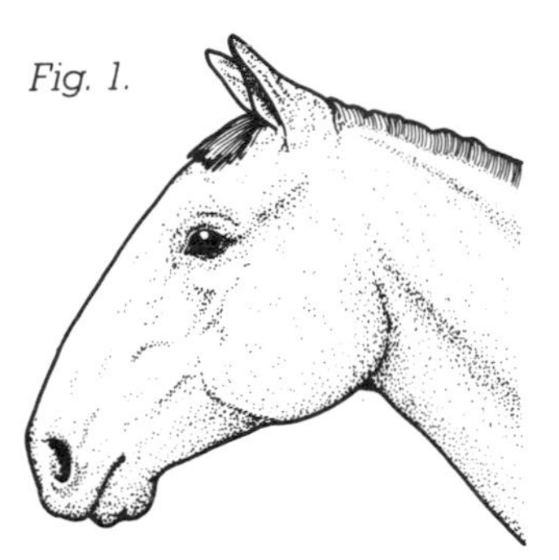

Roman nose

Dished face

Straight face

The conformation of the horse, i.e., the way it is 'put together', is a good indication of whether it will remain athletically sound. Animals with poor limb conformation put abnormal strains and stress on those limbs, which predisposes them to lameness.

The horse's body should be in proportion with the limbs and give an overall pleasant picture. Different breeds have differing characteristics in body shape and type, but they should still be well balanced whatever the breed specification. Well balanced means that the horse can be visually divided into three equal parts by drawing a perpendicular line from the point of the elbow to the withers and from the front of the stifle to the croup. The horse is then divided into head, neck and forelimb, body, and hind limb. A line taken from the point of the shoulder to the centre of the stifle will be parallel to the ground.

The head and neck balance the movement of the rest of the body. The head should not be excessively large nor the neck very short.

If the head is viewed from the side it may be straight, dished (concave) or roman nose (convex).

The forehead should be flat and broad with large eyes set on the side of the head.

The jaw should not have deformities like 'parrot mouth' or be 'undershot' as these give rise to dental problems and difficulties in eating.

Some horses are 'swan necked', i.e., the head meets the neck at an acute angle, or are very deep from the ear to the throat. Both conditions may cause respiratory

Fig. 2. Points of the horse

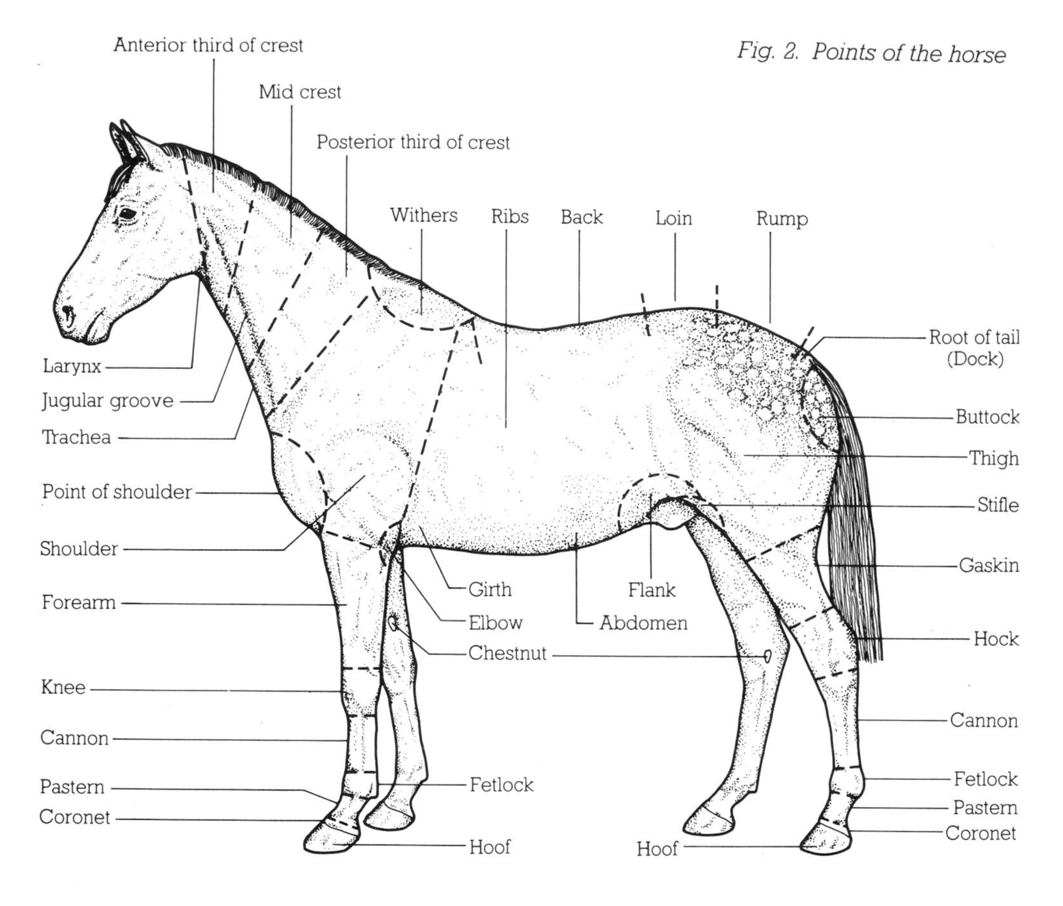

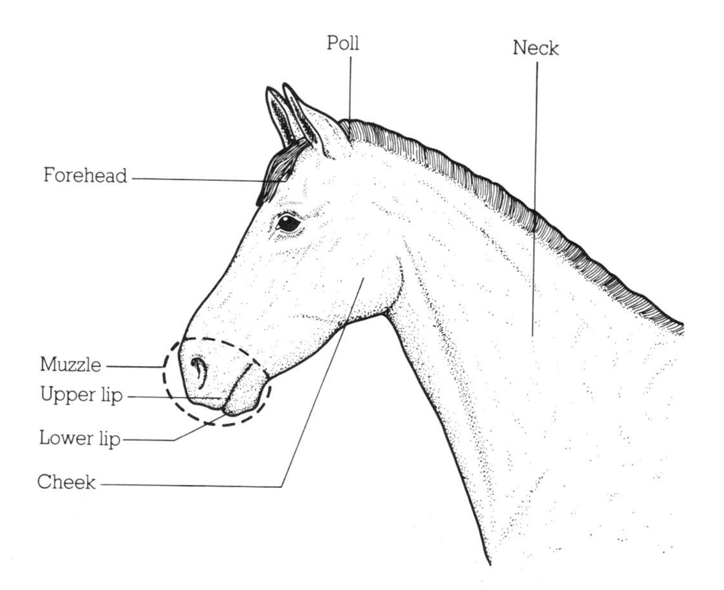

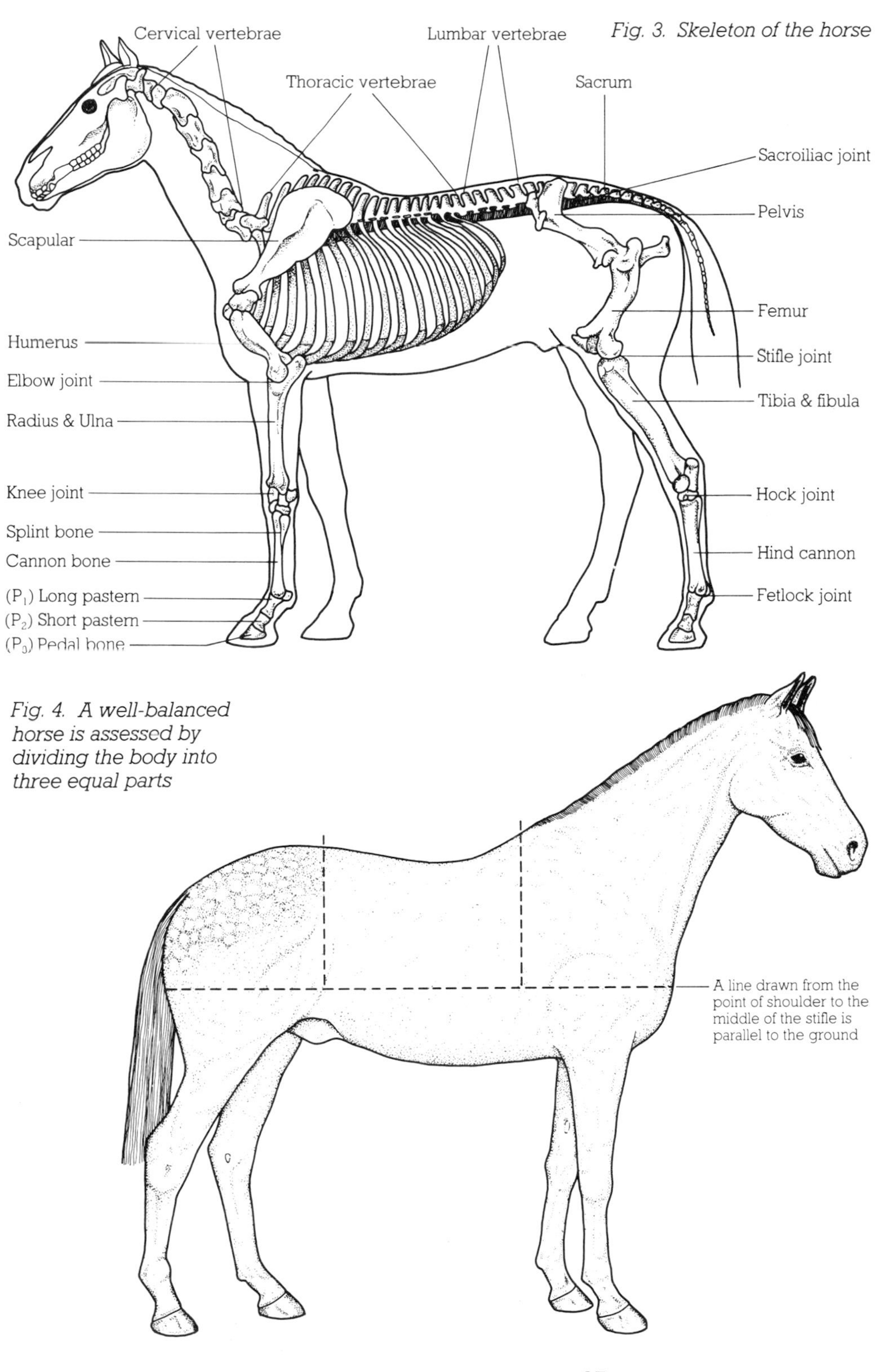

Fig. 3. Skeleton of the horse

Fig. 4. A well-balanced horse is assessed by dividing the body into three equal parts

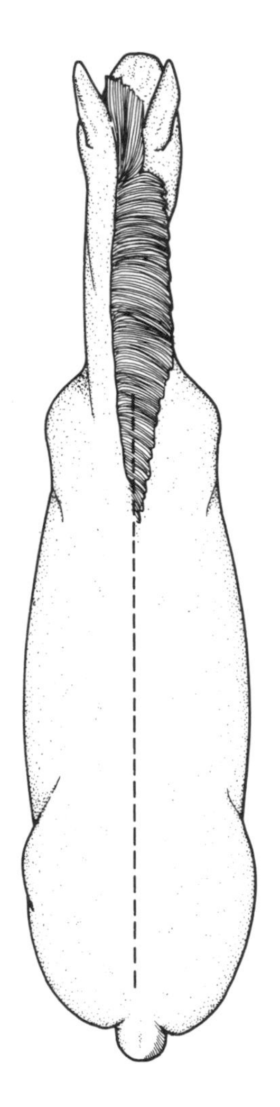

Fig. 5. A line drawn from the centre of the withers along the midline of the back divides the body into two equal parts

noises due to constriction of the larynx.

The neck should have an arched crest. It should be a good length with a slight dip in front of well-defined withers. The size of the crest and muscle development of the neck should be in proportion to the rest of the body. Stallions and very obese animals tend to be 'cresty'. 'Ewe necks' may be caused by poor conformation or poor riding, when a lot of muscle develops on the underside of the neck.

The withers are normally higher than the croup in an adult mature animal. Croup-high conformation brings the horse's centre of gravity further forward and puts more strain on the forelimbs.

It may be difficult to fit saddles on horses with high, narrow withers and on those with round shoulders and ill-defined withers. The saddle is difficult to keep in place in the latter case.

The slope (angle) of the shoulder-blade affects the amount of stress and concussion placed on the rest of the limb. Horses with longer, sloping shoulders can take longer strides. Those with short, upright shoulders take shorter, more frequent steps with more concussion and stress on the limbs.

The chest should be deep, well-developed and muscular with wide, well-sprung ribs to allow for good lung capacity. Horses with narrow chests and front legs close together frequently 'brush', i.e., the front legs interfere with each other to cause injury to the fetlocks.

If there is an abnormality in the straightness of the spine, it can often be seen. When viewed from above, a line drawn from the withers to the dock should divide the spine and the body into two equal parts.

3. *A pony with a 'cresty' neck.*

The spine should not curve to one side nor arch upwards, 'roach back', or dip downwards, 'sway back'.

Long-backed animals are weaker and prone to muscular and ligament strains, whereas short-backed horses are prone to vertebra injuries. If the latter is also long-legged, it may 'over reach', i.e., strike the heel or pastern of the front leg with the toe of the hind leg.

The horse should not be 'pot bellied' or 'herring gutted' (like a greyhound), but should have a gentle upward curve from the girth to the sheath or udder.

The hindquarters should be muscular and rounded with the point of the hips being symmetrical and a gradual slope from the croup to the dock.

Some horses have 'goose rumps', where the quarters slope acutely from the croup to the dock, while breeds such as Arabs have a flat croup.

THE LIMBS

The forelimbs of the horse bear 60–65 per cent of the body-weight and are subjected to more concussion than the hind limbs, which accounts for front leg lameness being commoner than hind leg lameness.

To assess the conformation of the limbs stand the horse on firm, level ground so that it is bearing weight on all its legs. First observe it from a distance, then examine it more closely at rest. Finally, watch it in walk and trot to assess its foot flight patterns and limb interference – do they move inwards or outwards, or do the legs hit each other.

Front Legs

Viewed from the front, the legs should be straight with both the toes pointing forward and bearing equal weight.

A perpendicular line from the point of the shoulder to the foot should divide the limb into equal halves.

Viewed from the side, a line dropped from the spine of the shoulder-blade should bisect the limb as far as the fetlock, the line hitting the ground just behind the heel.

Conformational faults of front legs

If the limb is not straight, abnormal strains will be

Fig. 6. Normal front leg, front view

Fig. 7. Normal front leg, side view

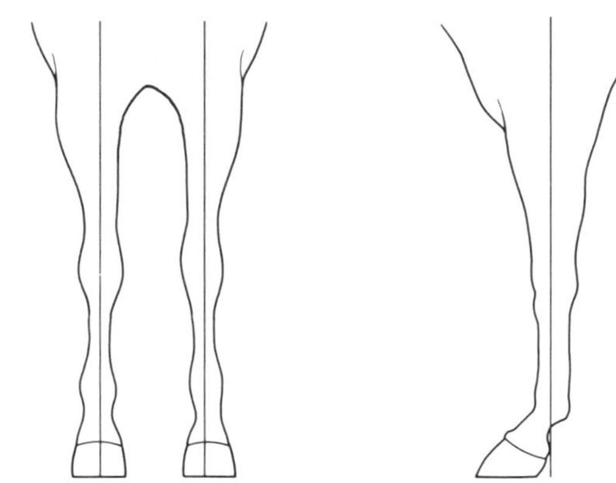

Fig. 8. Base narrow

Fig. 9. Base wide

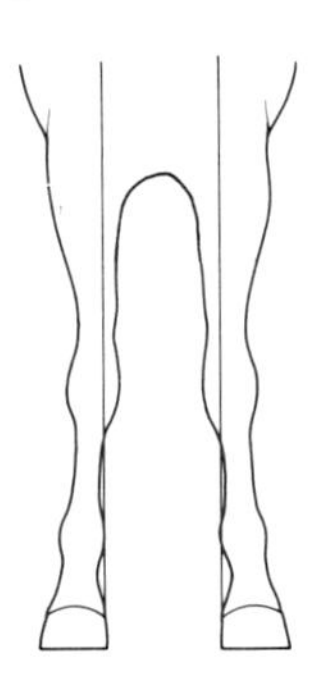

Fig. 10. Paddling

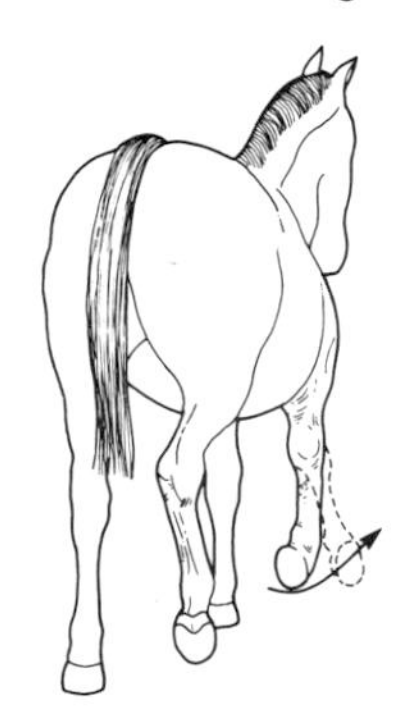

placed on the joints and the ligaments that bind them. The elbows should not turn inwards or outwards, and the knees should not deviate inwards (knock knees) or backwards (calf knees).

BASE NARROW

Horses with wide chests are frequently base narrow, i.e., the distance between the feet is less than the distance between the limbs at the chest. The horse takes more weight on the outside of the foot, and the lateral side of the limb is under more strain causing damage to the lateral side of the joints.

BASE WIDE

Narrow-chested horses are frequently base wide, i.e., the distance between the feet is greater than the distance between the limbs at the chest. The horse takes more weight on the inside (medial) of the foot and injures the medial ligaments and medial side of the joints.

These animals may have toe-in (pigeon toe) or toe-out (splay toe) conformation.

PIGEON TOE OR TOE IN

Pigeon-toed horses have toes that point inwards. The whole limb may turn inwards, or it may deviate only from low down, e.g. fetlock or pastern. As the horse moves, the foot usually swings outwards (paddles). If the limb deviates inwards at the pastern the foot may

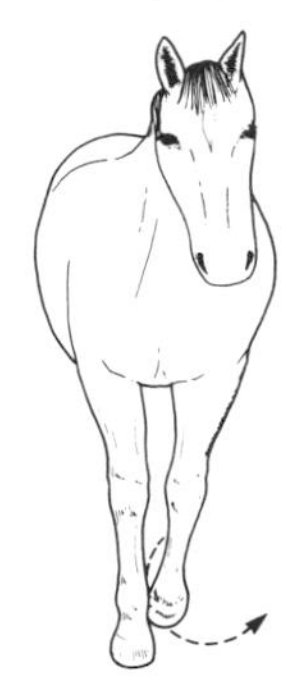
Fig. 11. Winging

swing inwards and so damage the opposite fetlock.

Pigeon toes are commoner in base-narrow horses.

SPLAY FOOT OR TOE OUT

Splay-footed horses have toes which point away from each other, i.e., outwards.

Often the deviation occurs high up in the limb. As the horse moves, the foot swings inwards (wings) and damages the opposite front leg, especially if the animal is also base narrow.

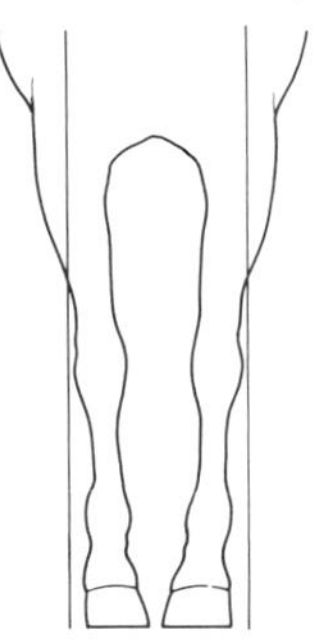
Fig. 12. Base narrow, toe in

BASE NARROW, TOE IN

Base narrow, toe in conformation causes strain on the lateral ligaments of the fetlock and the pastern joint's lateral sidebone and lateral ringbone. These animals usually have articular windgalls (distension of the fetlock joints). The outer wall of the foot will also be worn down, and the horse's feet paddle as it moves.

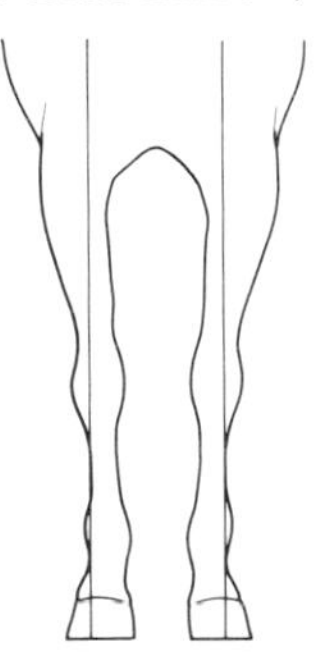
Fig. 13. Base narrow, toe out

BASE NARROW, TOE OUT

This is one of the worst conformational defects of the front legs. The foot lands on the outside wall, damaging the lateral side of the joints and placing a strain on the medial ligaments.

These horses tend to wing the foot inward and also plait the feet (put one foot immediately in front of the other), which causes interference injuries to the other leg, e.g., fracture of the medial splint bone. Plaiting also causes the horse to stumble, so making the animal dangerous to ride at speed!

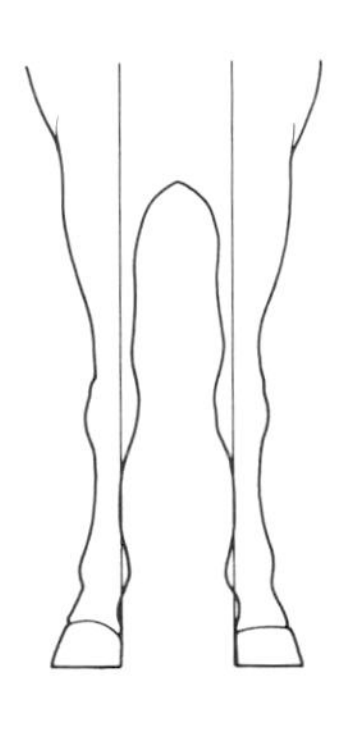
Fig. 14. Base wide, toe out

BASE WIDE, TOE OUT

Base-wide horses commonly have a toe-out conformation. This puts a strain on the medial ligaments and causes medial ringbone and sidebone and wear on the inside hoof wall. Fractures to the medial splint bone and cannon bone and injuries to the inside of the limbs from interference are common.

BASE WIDE, TOE IN

This conformation is very uncommon, but causes similar injuries to the inside of the limb as base-wide,

Fig. 15. Base wide, toe in

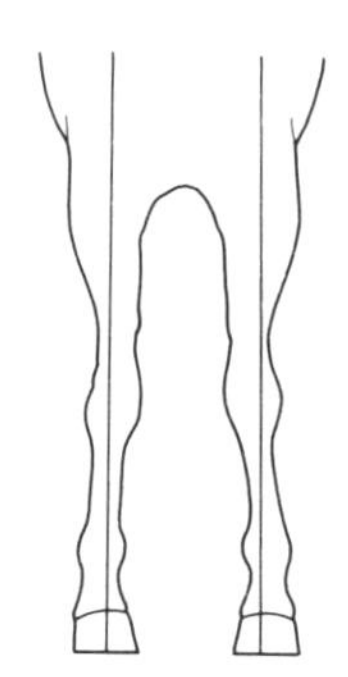

toe-out conformation. These horses usually paddle to the outside even though they land on the inside wall of the hoof.

Conformational defects of the knee (carpus)

OPEN KNEES

Indentations on the front of the knee are frequently seen in young animals but should not be present in adult animals. They are thought to be a weakness and make the joint more prone to injury.

Fig. 16. Open knees

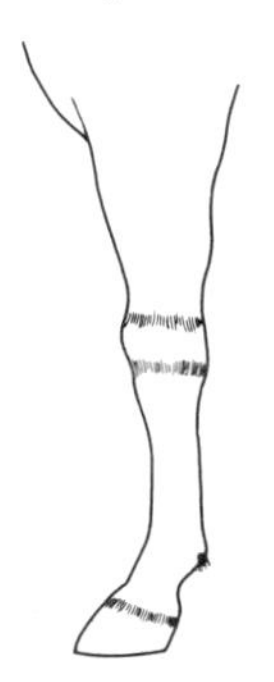

CALF KNEES

Knee joints which deviate backwards (calf knees), are a very bad fault as this places undue strain on the ligaments at the back of the carpus and injuries to the front of the carpal bones such as small (chip) fractures, when the limb is stressed by fast exercise.

Fig. 17. Calf knees

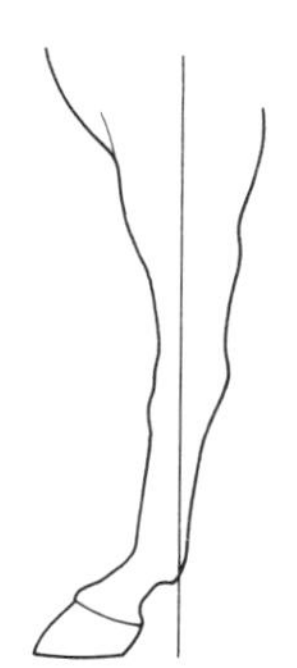

BUCKED KNEES
(OVER AT THE KNEE, OR GOAT KNEES)

This is a fairly common condition often seen in foals with contracted tendons. The knee joint deviates forward, placing strain on the flexors at the back of the leg. If the deviation is only slight it is less serious, only putting slight stress on the limb.

KNOCK KNEES

The knees are close together with some outward

Fig. 18. Bucked knees

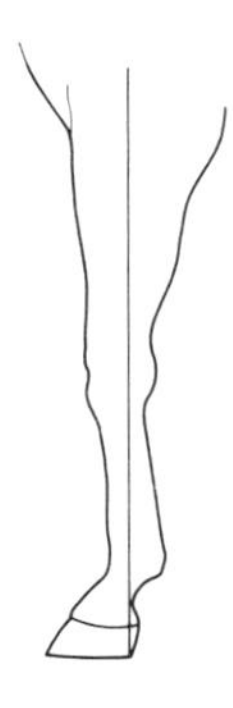

Fig. 19. Knock knees

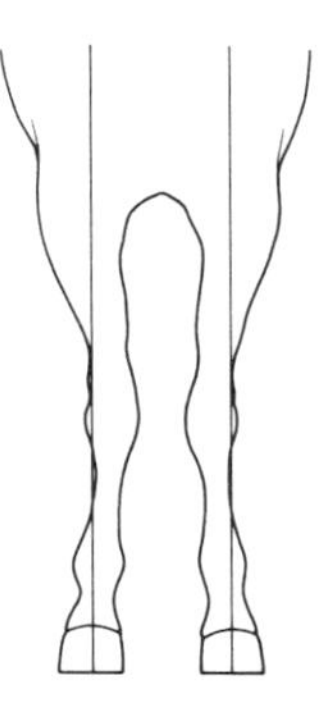

rotation of the lower limb. This puts a great strain on the medial ligaments of the carpus and compresses the carpal bones on the lateral side of the joint.

Fig. 20. Bow legs

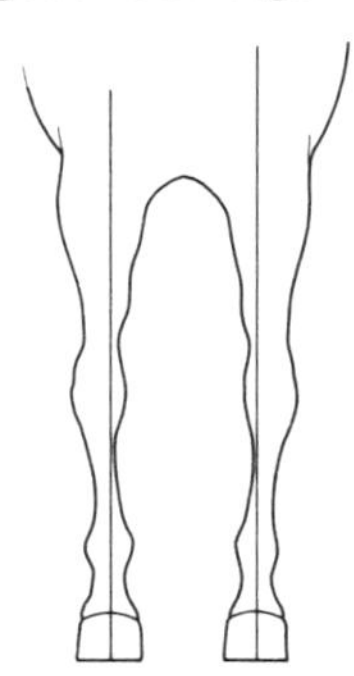

Fig. 21. Bench knees

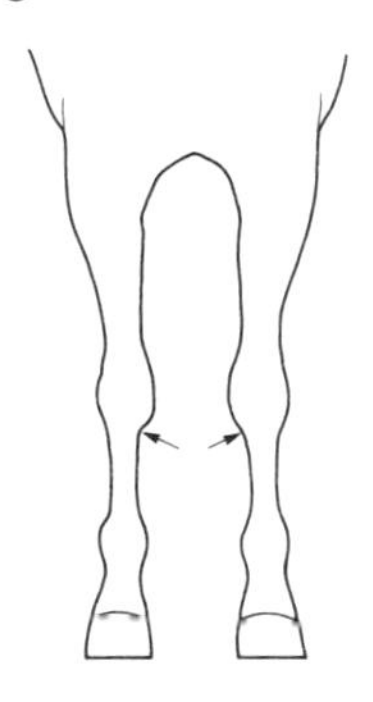

BOW LEGS

When viewed from the front, the legs bow out at the knees. This is often part of a base-narrow, toe-in conformation.

The lateral ligaments of the knee are strained and the carpal bones on the medial side of the joint are damaged by increased compression.

BENCH KNEES

The cannon bone should be placed under the carpus in line with the forearm (radius). A lateral (outside) deviation of the cannon bone is called 'bench knees'. The medial splint bone has a long, flat surface in contact with the carpus and so carries more weight than the lateral splint bone. In bench knees there is an even greater stress put on the medial splint bone, so a high incidence of 'splints' is seen in this condition. These occur due to damage to the ligament between the medial splint and the cannon bone.

Fig. 22. Tied-in knees

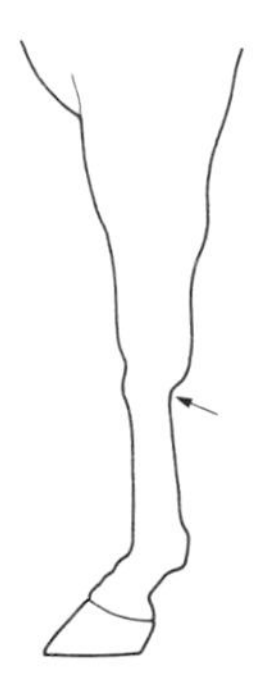

TIED-IN KNEES

The tendons at the back of the leg (flexors) appear to be too close to the cannon bone directly behind the knee. This prevents free movement.

CUT OUT UNDER THE KNEES

This is a weakness in conformation. When viewed from the side, there appears to be a 'cut-out' area below the knee joint on the cannon bone.

Fig. 23. Cut-out under knee

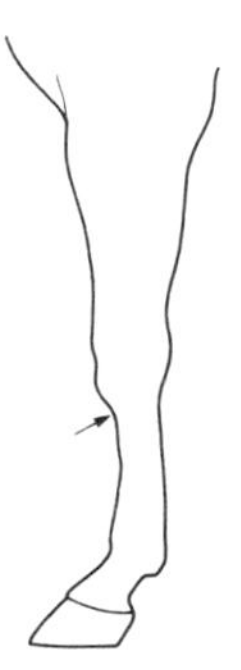

STANDING UNDER IN FRONT

When viewed from the side, the front legs seem to be further under the body than normal. This may be seen in certain diseases, e.g., laminitis when it affects all four feet.

This type of conformation leads to shorter strides and excessive wear and tear on the limbs. There is also an increased likelihood of stumbling.

Fig. 24. Standing under in front

Fig. 25. Camped in front

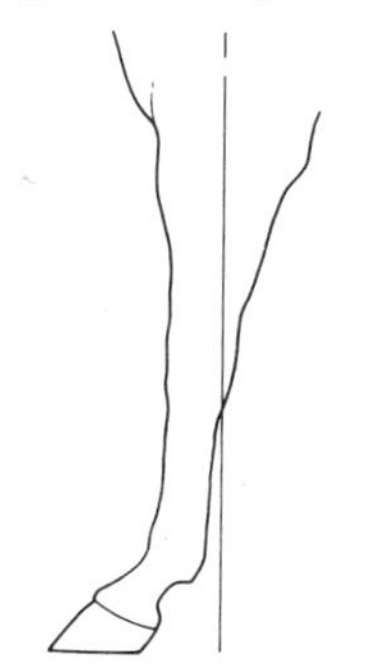

Fig. 26. Normal hoof pastern angle

Short upright pastern

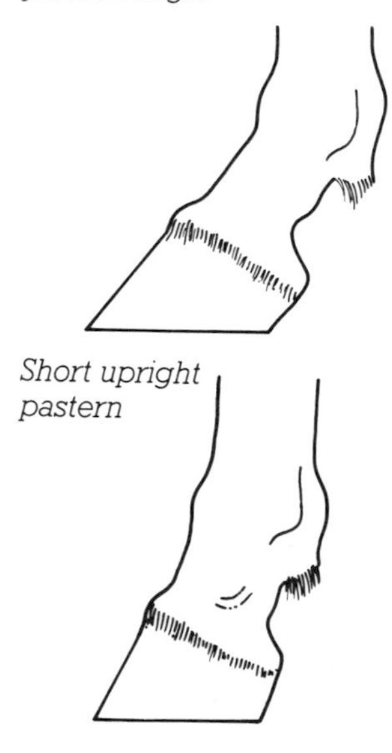

CAMPED IN FRONT

The front leg is way forward of its natural upright position when observed from the side. This is seen in navicular syndrome and front feet laminitis.

SHORT UPRIGHT PASTERNS

Horses with short upright pasterns increase the concussion on the fetlock and pastern joints and the navicular bone. Horses with straight shoulders that are base-narrow and toe-in often have this conformation. This predisposes to arthritis of the fetlock, pastern (ringbone) and navicular disease.

LONG SLOPING PASTERNS

The foot/pastern angle is less than normal (45°), putting undue strain on flexor tendons and suspensory ligament. The horse may injure the sesamoid bones at the back of the fetlock.

LONG UPRIGHT PASTERNS

This conformation predisposes to injuries of the fetlock joint and navicular bone as the long upright pastern has less anti-concussive properties than a sloping pastern.

The Hind Legs

To check the conformation of the hind legs, you should view them from behind and from the side with the animal standing square and its weight evenly distributed between the legs. The horse should then be observed walking and trotting to see if it has a straight leg action as with the front legs.

There is a lower incidence of hind-leg lameness compared to foreleg lameness. Poor hind-leg conformation predisposes to curbs, spavins and fixed patellas.

When viewed from behind, a vertical line dropped from the point of the buttocks should divide the entire limb into equal halves. The point of the hock being directly under the point of the buttocks. From the side, the line will continue down the back of the cannon bone and meet the ground just behind the heel. A horse with good hind-leg conformation will bear

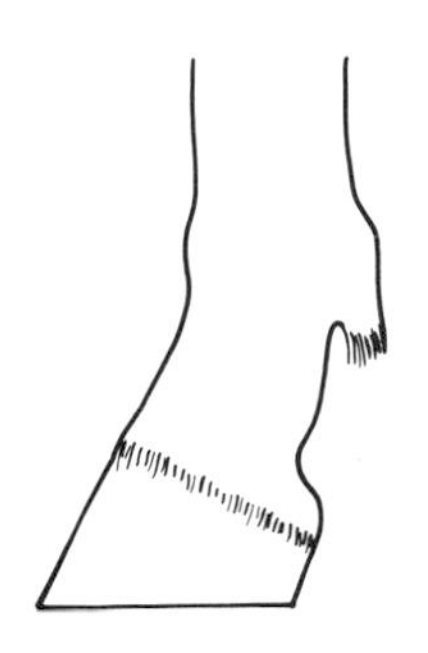
Fig. 27. Long upright pastern

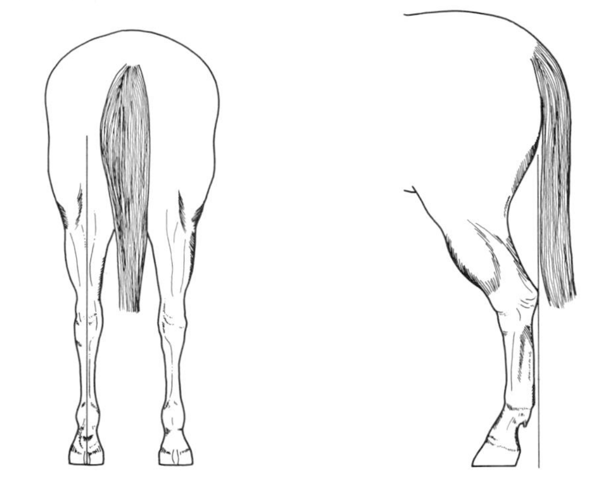
Fig. 28. Normal hind leg viewed from behind

Fig. 29. Normal hind leg viewed from the side

weight equally across the joints, so that the joints are compressed evenly. The ligaments on each side of the joint will bear equal strain.

The hocks should be large enough to take the weight of the horse and have a smooth outline (without any swellings) that tapers towards the cannon bone. The muscle of the thighs should not stop abruptly at the stifle, but continue down the tibia, tapering towards the hock.

The stifle and hock should not be too straight nor the hock be acutely angled. The hocks should not turn in towards each other nor bend away from each other.

Conformational faults of hind legs

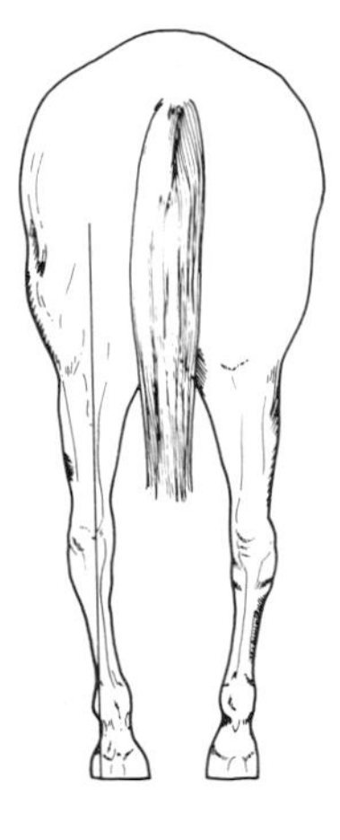
Fig. 30. Base narrow

BASE NARROW

Base narrow conformation occurs in well-muscled animals and those with bow legs and feet that toe in. The distance between the centre of the feet is smaller than the distance between the centre of the legs at the thighs. The weight is born on the outside wall of the foot with all the strain on the lateral side of the leg. The limb may be base narrow from the hock down, or the deviation may start higher up the leg. There may be interference between front and hind legs.

BASE WIDE

When viewed from behind the distance between the

centre of the feet is greater than the distance between the centre of the limbs at the thigh.

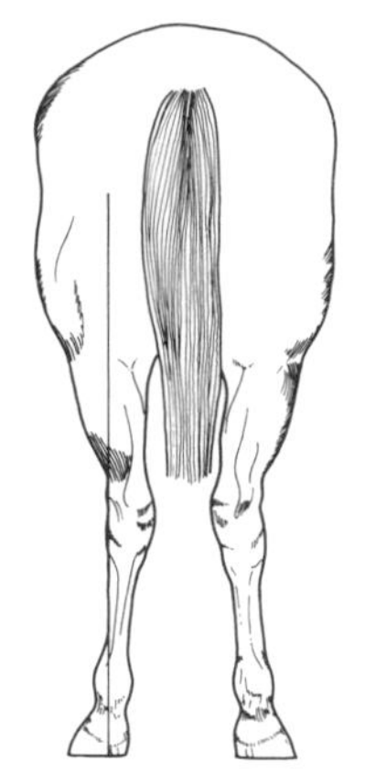

Fig. 31. Cow hocks

COW HOCKS

A horse with cow hocks has legs that are base-narrow as far as the hocks, and then base wide from the hocks to the feet, which usually toe out.

Many animals are slightly cow-hocked without any adverse effects on their way of going, provided that they have no other conformational fault.

Cow-hock conformation puts extra stress on the inside of the hock joint, which may lead to bone spavin (osteoarthritis or degenerative joint disease (DJD) of the hock joint).

Fig. 32. Standing under behind

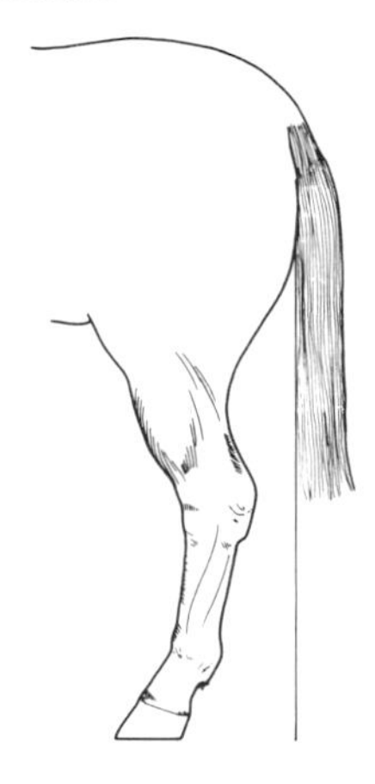

SICKLE HOCKS

A horse with sickle hocks stands with its hind feet placed too far forward (i.e., under the body) from the hock down, so the angle of the hock is too acute. This can cause bog spavin (fluid distension of the hock joint capsule), bone spavin, and because of the strain on the plantar ligament, which runs down the back of the leg, curbs may form (a thickening of the plantar ligament and the underlying bone).

If a horse is both sickle and cow hocked, it is unlikely to remain athletically sound if given any real work.

Fig. 33. Sickle hocks

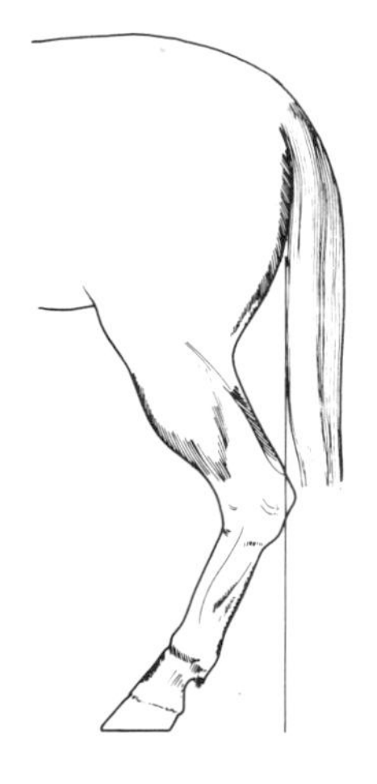

STRAIGHT HIND LEGS

If the stifle and hock joints are too straight, this puts a strain on the front of the hock joint capsule, resulting in a 'bog spavin'. It can also cause a 'locking' knee cap (patella) due to the straightness of the stifle. This condition is common in animals which are poorly muscled and are long from stifle to hock.

Straight-legged horses tend to have upright pasterns and are often 'camped behind' (the whole leg is placed too far behind the body).

Large, hard swellings on the head of the lateral (outside) splint bone are sometimes confused with curbs. These are called false curbs and are blemishes.

Soft swellings on either side of the large flexor tendon above the point of the hock are 'thoroughpins'. These are distensions of the tarsal sheath which surrounds the tendon.

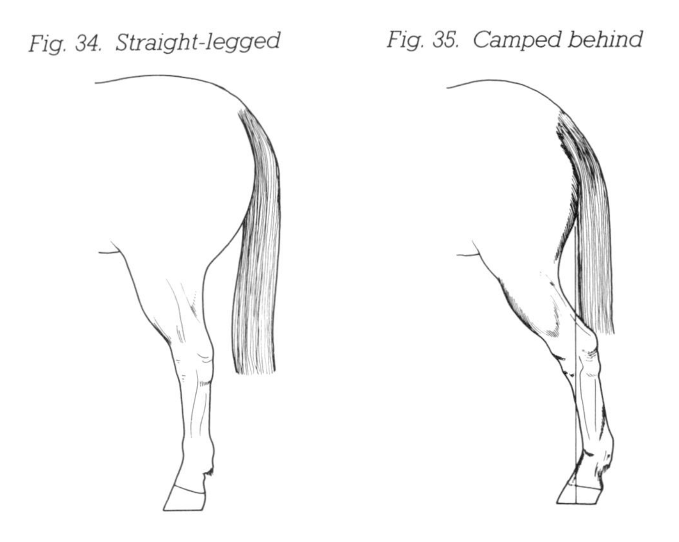

Fig. 34. Straight-legged *Fig. 35. Camped behind*

The Foot

A horse with poor limb conformation will have poor foot conformation, especially if the foot is landing unevenly. This is evident by uneven wear on the walls of the foot.

The front foot should be round and wide at the heels with a wall of adequate thickness to bear the weight of the animal. The normal wall is thickest at the

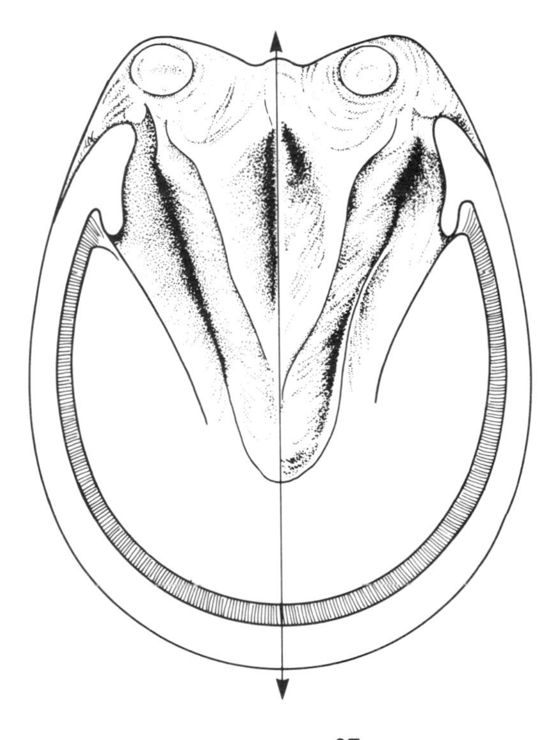

Fig. 36. An imaginary line drawn through the central groove of the frog, the point of the frog and the toe clip of the front shoe should divide the foot into equal halves

Fig. 37. A broken foot pastern axis

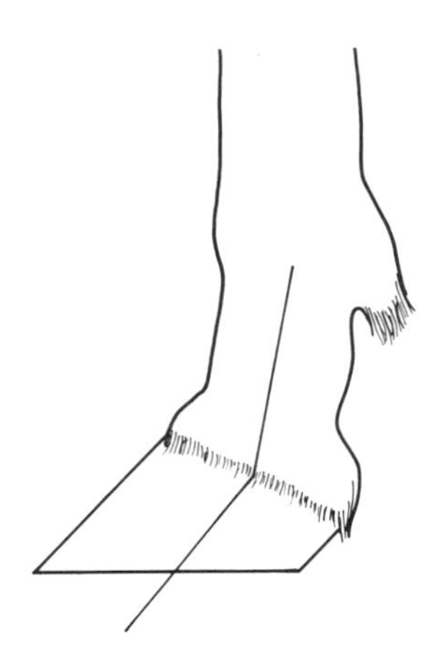

toe, with the inside wall being straighter than the outside. The sole is concave and thick enough to prevent bruising. A line drawn through the centre of the heels and apex of the frog to the toe should divide the foot into equal halves.

The hind foot has a more pointed appearance and the sole is more concave than the front foot. When viewed from the side, the angle the wall of the foot makes with the ground (foot axis) is 45–50° for the front feet and 50–55° for the hind feet. This should be continuous with the slope of the pastern and is called the foot–pastern axis.

If the slope of the hoof wall (foot axis) differs from the slope of the pastern (pastern axis), this broken-foot pastern axis has to be corrected by the farrier. Usually the foot is trimmed or shod to correct the foot axis.

The hoof should have outside and inside walls of the same length, i.e., the foot should be level.

Faults in Foot Conformation

FLAT FEET

Horses with flat feet are frequently lame due to the pain from bruised soles. This is commoner in the front feet than hind feet. To avoid extra pressure on the soles the horse tends to land on its heels.

DROPPED SOLE

Dropped soles are usually a result of laminitis (see page 44). The sole may appear convex and is below the level of the walls. It will be thicker and flakier than normal and show signs of bruising (haemorrhage). In severe cases, the tip of the pedal bone will penetrate the sole in front of the point of the frog. This is due to rotation of the pedal bone as the laminae are torn apart.

Any animal with a dropped sole is unlikely to remain sound enough for athletic use and will need expert veterinary attention and constant care from the farrier.

CONTRACTED FOOT

A contracted foot is one that is narrower and smaller

than normal. The whole foot may be involved or just the heels. Horses with navicular disease often have contracted heels.

The sole of a contracted foot will be more concave (dished) and the frog will be small.

If the horse is not weight-bearing on a foot it will become contracted. This may be due to pain in the foot or higher up the limb. Poor shoeing may also result in foot contraction. Excessive drying of the feet may also cause them to contract.

CLUB FOOT

Club feet are usually inherited or due to dietary factors but if only one foot is involved this may be secondary to an injury or contraction of the flexor tendons. A club foot has a steep foot axis (60°+) which makes the horse likely to stumble.

THIN WALLS AND SOLES

Horses inherit thin walls and soles. These animals will be prone to lameness due to excessive wearing down of the walls and bruising of the sole.

The horse may be left unshod to encourage the walls to grow and sole to harden up. Over a period of time the condition of the wall and sole may improve.

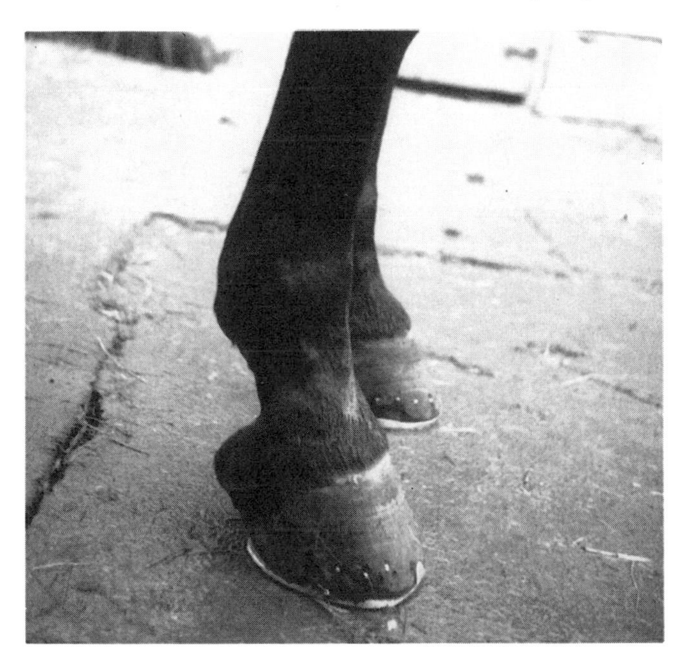

4. Contracted high heels on a narrow foot.

SECTION 2
PRACTICAL HEALTH CARE

CHAPTER 4
BODY CONDITION

The horse's body condition is a reflection of its diet, the amount of exercise it gets, and its state of health. Condition can also be affected by external environmental factors such as climate and grazing companions.

The body condition can vary from grossly overweight to emaciated, depending on the amount of fat under the skin. Most obese animals are given too much food and too little exercise. Some horses put on weight very easily, and so the conscientious owner has to restrict the daily intake of food and frequently check the body-weight. It is hard to convince some owners that their horse is overweight, and even harder to persuade them to put the horse on a diet. The trend towards obese show animals, however, is at last losing favour with the more knowledgeable judges and discerning owners.

The commonest reason for a horse to be in a lean condition is because its feed is insufficient, in both quantity and quality. Sharp cheek teeth, internal parasites, inadequate shelter from adverse weather conditions and bullying in the field will all contribute to a horse's being in a poor condition.

Many owners fail to notice changes in the horse's body-weight unless they are very pronounced, and the animal may be under- or over-fed for a long time. However, there are ways of monitoring the horse's body-weight and condition so that fluctuations in weight can be prevented. Once the horse is at its optimum weight for performance, it is then a matter of keeping it at that weight by making small adjustments to the dietary intake. Condition-scoring (see page 32) is an excellent way to monitor the horse's response to changes in feed intake.

ESTIMATING BODY-WEIGHT

The easiest way to monitor a gain or loss in weight is to measure the exact girth circumference each week. The horse could be weighed on a public weighbridge or on a weighbridge especially designed for livestock. This would give an accurate body-weight. Unfortunately, few people have access to weighbridges.

There are methods of estimating body-weight that do not involve expensive equipment or a great deal of time, and which are simple to perform. Using a metric fibre tape-measure, measure the horse's length from the point of the shoulder to the point of the buttocks. Then measure the heart girth circumference immediately behind the elbow as the horse breathes out. Hold the tape firmly while doing this. In order to be accurate, two people should hold the tape when measuring the length of the horse.

The body-weight can then be calculated in the following way.

$$\text{Formula: weight (kg)} = \frac{\text{girth cm}^2 \times \text{length cm}}{Y}$$

$Y = 11880\ \text{cm}^3/\text{kg}$

13.3 hh pony cob type heart girth = 172 cm
length = 145 cm

$$\text{Therefore, weight in kg} = \frac{172 \times 172 \times 145}{11880}$$

$$= \frac{4289680}{11880}$$

$= 361$ kg

On a weigh-bridge this pony weighed 360 kg.

The body-weight can also be calculated using height measurements with condition-scoring (see page 35).

The horse's height can be accurately measured at the highest point of the withers with the animal unshod and standing square on level ground. The head should be in a normal position, i.e., eye-level above the wither-level. A standard measuring stick as used by most vets is more accurate than a tape-measure.

CONDITION-SCORING

Condition-scoring involves assessing the amount of fat deposited in three different areas of the body: the neck, the back and ribs, and the pelvis. These areas are examined visually and by palpation (gently pinching with the fingers to see how much flesh there is under the coat). The horse's condition is then assessed on a scale of 0 to 5, where 0 = emaciated and 5 = very obese, using Table 1.

View the pelvis from behind and assess visually the amount of flesh covering the bones. Then palpate the pelvis and croup, because in the case of a very hairy animal it is difficult to assess the condition just by sight. Horses in a poor condition will have a deep depression under the tail and little flesh on the inner thighs. The pelvis will appear angular and the flanks hollow. A

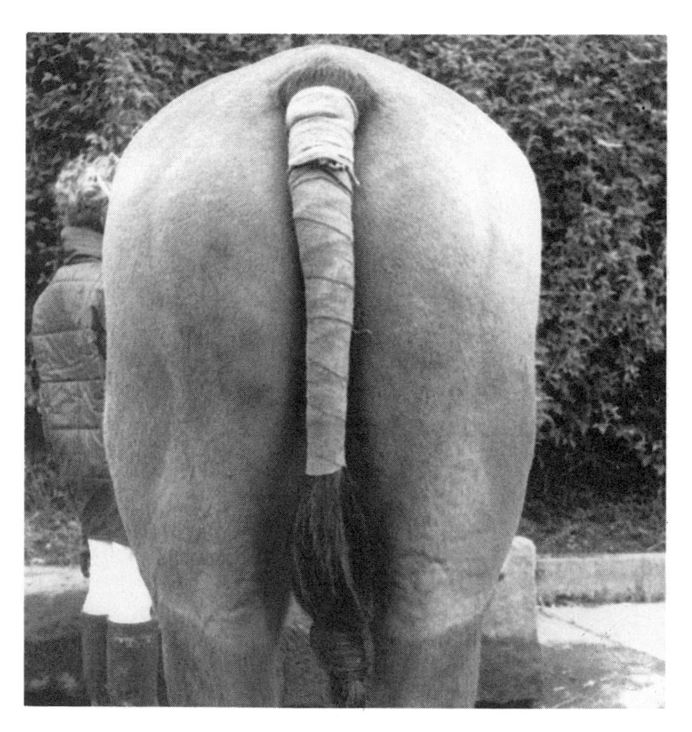

5. Condition-scoring the horse by viewing the pelvis from behind. 2.5 score.

	0 = Emaciated	1 = Poor	2 = Fair/ Moderate	3 = Good	4 = Fat	5 = Very obese
Neck	Marked ewe neck	Ewe neck	No top line	Top line good but not cresty (except stallions)	Slight crest. Folds of fat starting.	Marked crest. Folds of fat very obvious.
	Base of neck narrow & slack	Narrow and slack at base	Narrow but firm	Firm	Wide & firm.	Very wide & firm.
Ribs & Back	Skin drawn tight over ribs easy to feel & see	Ribs clearly visible	Ribs just visible. Back bone covered.	Ribs & vertebrae covered. Ribs can be easily felt.	Ribs well covered – only felt on firm pressure	Ribs buried in fat & cannot be felt
	Backbone sharp and easily seen	Vertebrae well defined & sharp to touch	Vertebrae easily felt.	No gutter along back	Gutter along backbone	Deep gutter along back. Back like a table.
Pelvis	Bone structure visible – Angular pelvis– Skin tight. Deep cavity under tail, hollow flanks, no muscle between hind legs.	Pelvis & crcup well defined. Deep depression under tail. Skin supple.	Rump flat. Each side of spine croup well defined. Pelvis easily felt. Cavity under tail.	Pelvis covered by fat so rounder appearance. No gutter. Pelvis can be felt. Smooth skin.	Pelvis well covered, only felt with firm pressure. Gutter at root of tail.	Pelvis buried, cannot feel any part of it. Deep gutter at root of tail. Skin distended.

6. Condition score 4. This pony also has sweetitch – note the rubbed tail.

horse in a very obese condition will have a round rump with a deep gutter at the base of the tail and the inner thighs will be in close contact.

To condition-score the neck, it is best to stand at the horse's shoulder and feel just in front of the withers, at the base of the neck, to assess the firmness and width. Study the shape of the neck. Some horses with poor conformation have ewe necks. Those that are not schooled tend to have a poor top line but are not necessarily in poor condition.

A very overweight horse will have a huge crest with folds of fat at the base of the neck. It is quite normal for stallions to be cresty, so the other areas of the body would have to be checked for condition before a judgement of overweight was given.

The third place to score is the ribs and backbone. Stand at the horse's side to check if the ribs and vertebrae are visible. Then palpate these areas to assess the amount of flesh covering them. Very fat horses have a gutter running along the midline of the backbone. The back is like a table-top in these animals, and it is impossible to feel the ribs even with firm pressure.

If the pelvis score differs by 1 or more points from the neck or back scores, adjust it by 0.5 to give the actual condition score.

EXAMPLE 1

Pelvis	Back	Difference	Adjustment	Condition score
3	2	−1	0.5	2.5
	Neck			
	3	0	—	

EXAMPLE 2

Pelvis	Back	Difference	Adjustment	Condition score
3	2	−1	—	
	Neck			
	4	+1	—	3

If the condition score and height of the horse are known, the weight can be calculated using a condition score/height measurement nomogram (after Carroll and Huntington, 1988).

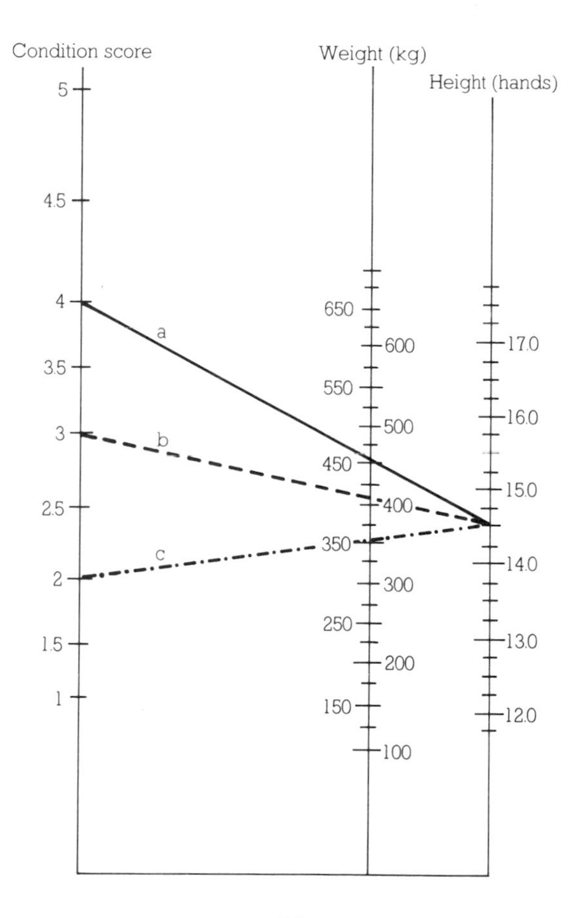

Fig. 38. Nomogram for estimating bodyweight from height and condition score

a. 14.2 hh horse with condition score 4 weighs 450 kg.

b. 14.2 hh horse with condition score 2 weighs 350 kg.

c. 14.2 hh horse with condition score 3 weighs 410 kg.

CHAPTER 5
FOOT CARE

STRUCTURE OF THE FOOT

The hoof is a horny box that surrounds the bones of the foot, the ligaments which bind the bones together, the tendons from the muscles higher up the leg, and the subcutaneous tissues, blood vessels and nerves. It consists of a modified epidermis (outer layer of skin), which corresponds to human finger-nail, and the coronary band from which the horn tubules grow, is similar to cuticle. It is divided into the wall (the part which is visible when the horse's foot is bearing weight), and the sole (the under-surface of the foot).

The wall is thickest at the toe, becoming gradually thinner and more elastic over the quarters to the heel. This allows the heel to expand when bearing weight. At the heel, the wall turns inwards onto the sole to

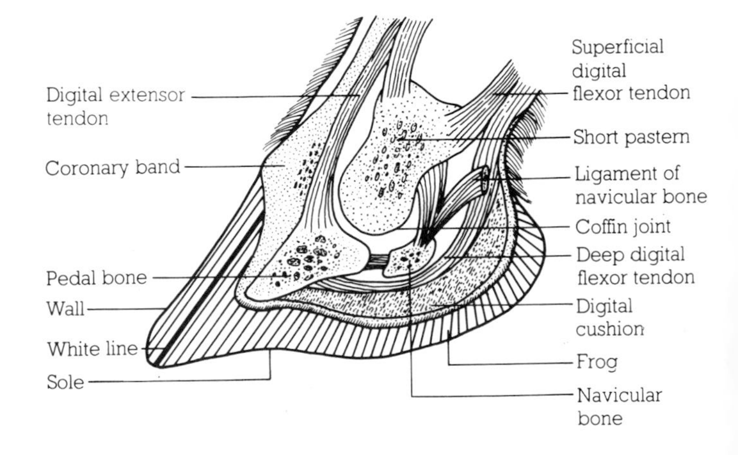

Fig. 39. Section through the foot

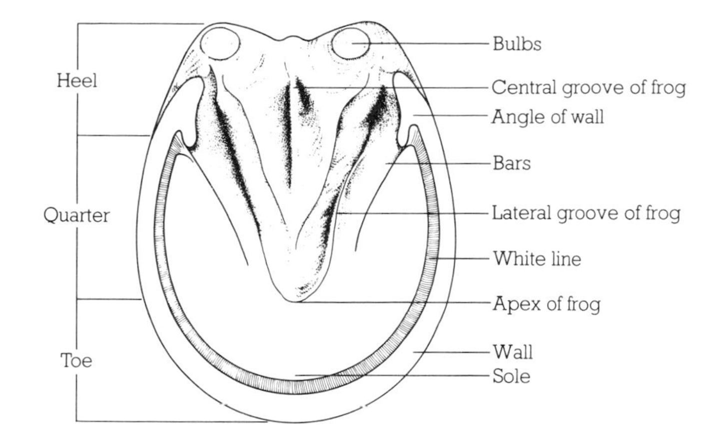

Fig. 40. Normal forefoot showing the structures of the solar surface

form the bars. These are separated by grooves from the softer and more elastic triangular frog. The frog has a central groove.

The sole is concave (dished). This is more obvious in the hind feet and in unshod (bare-foot) horses, and helps to prevent the sole being bruised. The horn of the sole is more flakey and softer than the wall horn due to its higher water content. Under the sole and frog lies the elastic digital cushion which acts as a shock absorber and supports the bulbs of the heels.

The hoof wall has three layers. The smooth and glossy outer layer is a very thin layer of tubular horn that reduces moisture loss from the foot. On its surface are parallel lines from the coronary band right down to the ground-bearing surface. These show the direction of growth of the horn. Any ridges are due to changes in growth rate caused by a change to the horse's diet, or perhaps by weather conditions. The hoof grows fastest in warm and moist conditions. The middle layer of the hoof wall is very thick and pigmented. The inner layer consists of hundreds of laminae (leaves), which intermesh with the sensitive laminae on the surface of the pedal bone. The white line is the lighter, softer band of horn on the solar (ground) surface dividing the wall horn from the sole horn. This is used as a guide when nailing on metal shoes.

Three bones make up the skeleton of the foot. The pedal bone (third or distal phalanx) is semi-circular in the front feet and oval in the hind feet. The small bone at the back of the pedal bone is called the navicular (distal sesamoid) bone which forms a joint with it and the short pastern (middle or second phalanx). The

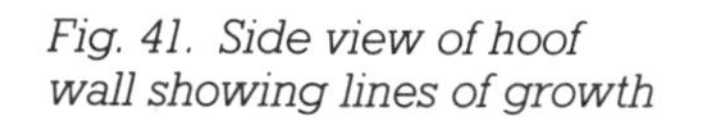

Fig. 41. Side view of hoof wall showing lines of growth

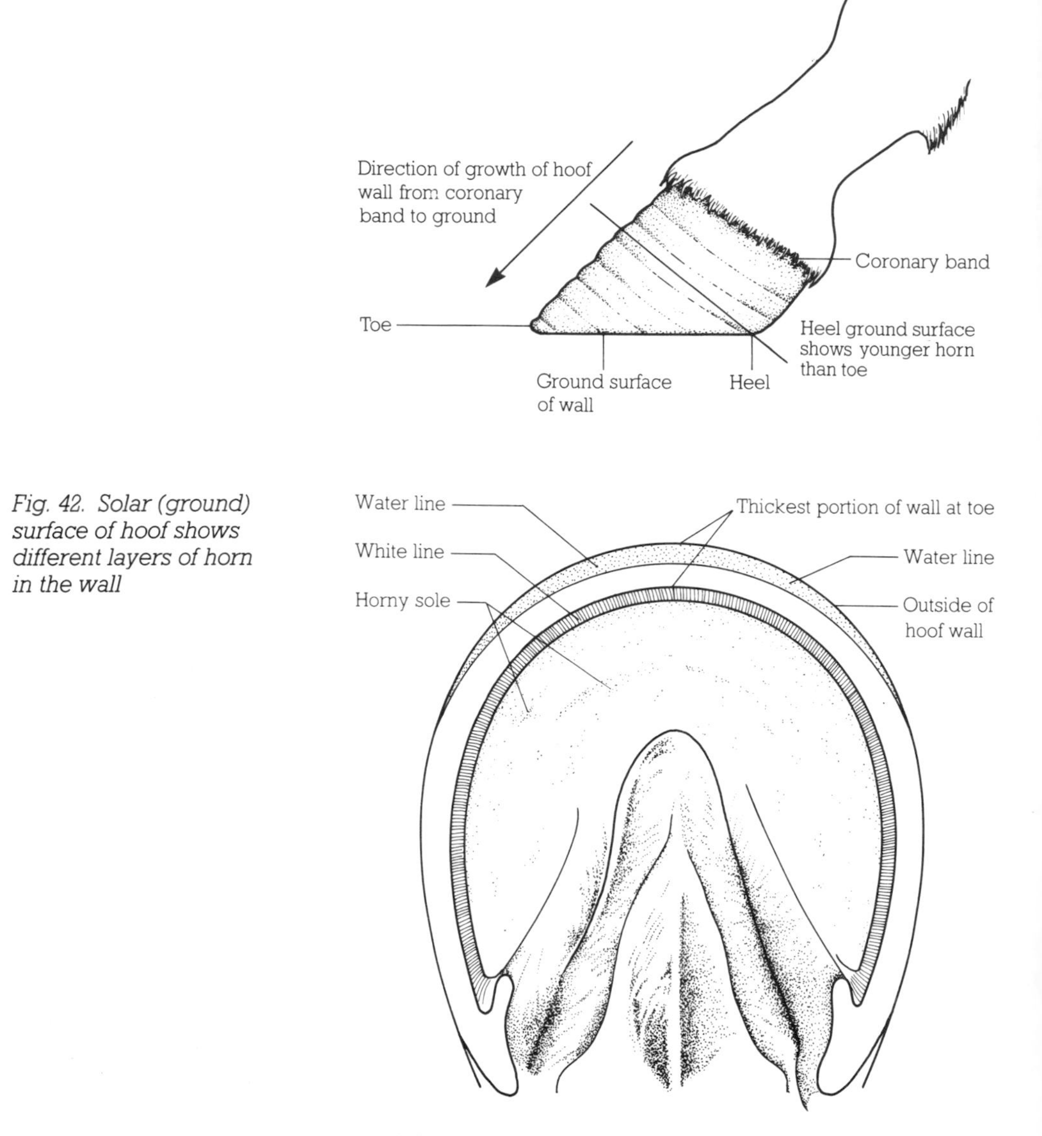

Fig. 42. Solar (ground) surface of hoof shows different layers of horn in the wall

pedal bone is covered with highly vascular laminae that intermesh with those of the inner layer of the hoof wall. These laminae bear the weight of the horse.

DAILY ROUTINE – PICKING OUT THE FEET

A lot of veterinary time is spent examining lame horses, the majority of which have a lower limb or foot problem. Some of the common conditions could be prevented or recognized in their early stages if proper attention was paid to the feet. Remember: no foot – no horse!

Pick out the feet carefully every day in the same sequence, with the horse tied up and standing square. This is important in training the young horse and owner! As you pick out the feet, look for the following signs of problems.

Check the temperature of each hoof. The temperature of the hoof wall may vary with external conditions, but usually all four feet feel the same. Heat in a foot is a sign of infection or injury.

Once the sole, wall and frog grooves are clean, check the hoof for damage, such as cracks or defects in the wall, puncture holes, soft areas on the sole.

If the horse is kept on a dirty, wet bed or in a waterlogged field, the frog tends to flatten and mushroom out over the grooves which then become underrun (infected) and soft. There may be an

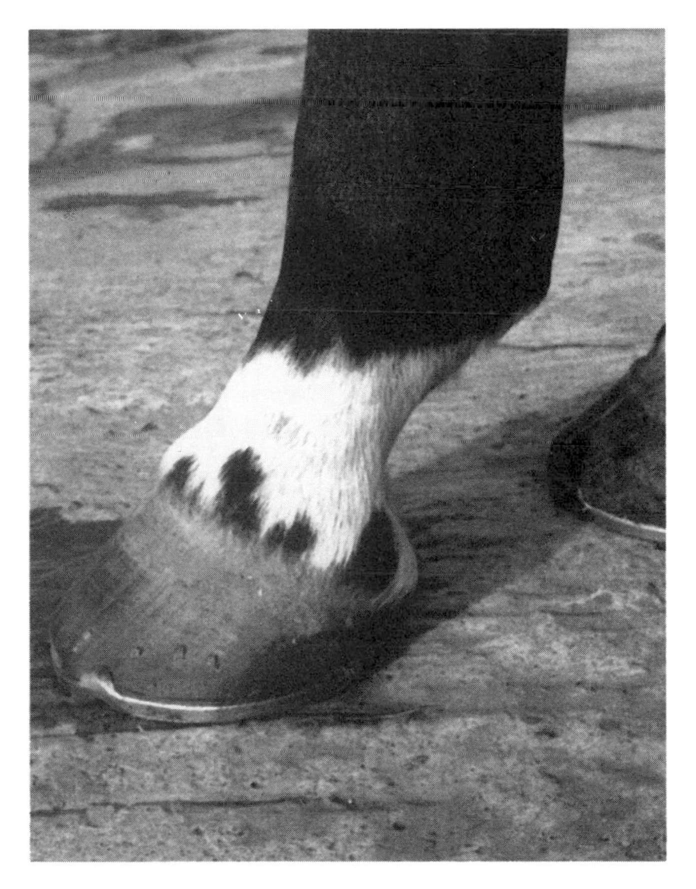

7. Check the feet and shoes daily. Here the clenches have started to lift.

offensive black discharge in the grooves. This disease, **thrush**, can be prevented by improving the conditions underfoot and correctly paring the frog.

The farrier usually trims the frog so that it is in contact with the ground (when the foot is weight-bearing) and the grooves remain well defined and aerated.

As the hoof grows, the shoe moves forward off the wall at the heel and onto the sole towards the bars. The sole becomes bruised and may result in a painful corn. Stones, pieces of wood or metal may become lodged in the gap between the shoe and the wall. If the clenches are raised they may damage the opposite leg. The foot needs trimming and the shoe resetting if any of these conditions arise.

A shoe which has worn thin in one area is a sign that the foot is not landing flat. This alteration in gait may be due to pain somewhere in that limb. For example, wear on the toe of a front shoe is often due to pain in the back of the foot.

Frequently, a nail or a sharp object becomes embedded in the foot. Before this is removed, its angle, depth and position must be assessed. If the penetration is in the middle or back third of the foot, the vital structures around the navicular bone, coffin joint and deep flexor tendon may be involved. Infection introduced into these sites is extremely difficult to treat and very serious.

If the horse can bear weight on the foot without forcing the nail deeper into the foot, call the vet and let him remove the nail. If the animal cannot stand,

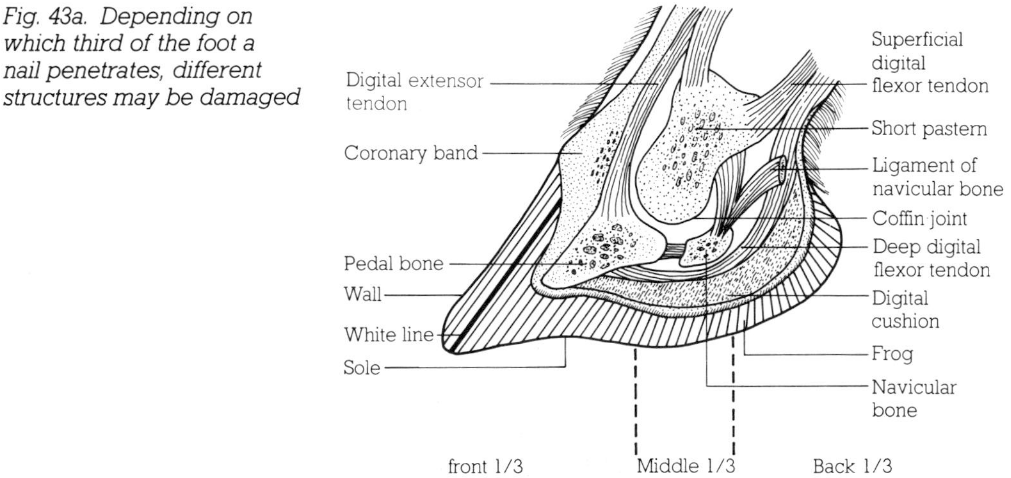

Fig. 43a. Depending on which third of the foot a nail penetrates, different structures may be damaged

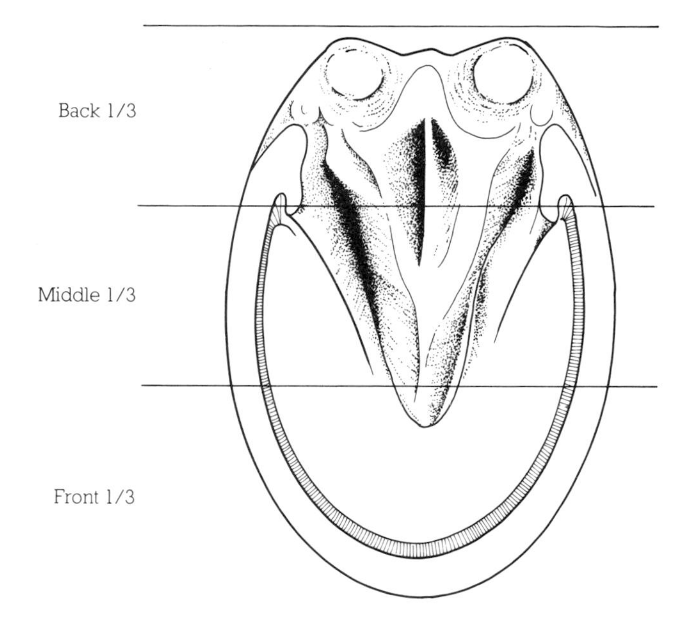

Fig. 43b. A normal hind foot divided into thirds. This method is used to assess the position of a penetrating foreign body within the foot

remove the nail yourself but remember how deep into the tissue it went. If possible, mark the foot to show the position of the puncture hole. Depending on how long you have to wait for professional assistance, it may be necessary to apply a foot dressing (see bandages, poultices and barrier boots, pages 128, 131).

Check the bulbs of the heels and the pastern for injuries while you have the foot held up. Damage to the coronary band is serious if the horn-producing cells are injured. This can lead to a defect in the horn below the injury for the rest of the animal's life. This deformed horn may not be able to bear weight when it reaches the ground surface; it may also be unsuitable for nailing into to hold on a shoe.

Remember that you do not pick out the horse's feet just to please the person who brushed the yard.

HOOF DRESSINGS

Horn quality varies with climate, diet, the horse's general state of health and the conditions underfoot. In addition, horn growth slows down in cold, dry conditions and increases in a warm, moist climate. It is therefore difficult to assess the beneficial effect, if any, of a particular hoof dressing.

Excessive moisture makes the hoof weak and more

pliable, the sole becomes thicker and flatter, and the toes longer. The heels and quarters collapse and the walls flare and separate, so the hoof loses its efficient shape. Minerals may be leached out of the hoof by excessive moisture.

In very dry weather the hoof tends to become hard and brittle, the sole flakey and the ground surface of the walls prone to cracks. These may be **grass** or **sand cracks** and can occur at the toe, quarter or heel. They may extend from the coronary band to the ground surface, or start at the bearing surface of the wall and only extend a short way up the wall. Corrective trimming and shoeing is necessary to prevent a small grass crack becoming a long and wide defect in the wall. If cracks are neglected they may penetrate the sensitive tissues, and the ensuing infection will result in a lame horse.

Full-length cracks are due to a defect at the coronary band and will be present for the entire life of the horse. Surgical shoeing may be needed to prevent the crack from opening up and exposing the deeper layers of the wall.

The ideal hoof dressing should protect the hoof from any adverse or extreme environmental conditions and maintain good horn quality. There are numerous types, all of which claim to keep the hoof healthy, supple and resilient. Some have a purely cosmetic effect, leaving the hoof wall shiny, while others are supposed to increase the growth-rate of the horn. They vary in cost, time taken to apply and effectiveness.

Most brands are in the form of either oils, which are messy, or waxes and creams, which are spill-proof but hard to apply in cold weather. The newest coating agents (sealants) give a high-gloss, long-lasting finish, and are supposed to strengthen the hoof wall and replace the periople (the outer layer of the hoof wall), the function of which is to reduce water loss by evaporation. Oils and waxes waterproof the hoof so may also be beneficial in wet conditions, and coating agents seal out moisture from the environment and prevent the hoof becoming waterlogged.

Excessive moisture can be removed from the feet prior to waterproofing them by standing the horse in a dry shavings bed. Dry, brittle feet should be thoroughly soaked in water before using any waterproofing agent.

Hard feet can be successfully softened by poulticing. This is extremely useful when the hoof has to be pared out, as in cases of infection. Over-zealous use of poultices can cause a very soggy and smelly foot, so beware!

FEEDING TO IMPROVE HORN GROWTH AND QUALITY

There are a number of causes of poor-quality hooves and slow horn growth. A horse on an inadequate plane of nutrition with a poor condition-score will have slow horn growth of poor quality, as will an animal suffering from a chronic debilitating disease. Some horses inherit thin walls and soles that are prone to cracking and bruising. Often horses that are in good bodily condition, healthy and with no history of disease have brittle, thin horn which crumbles around the nail holes and on the ground surface of the walls. In these horses, cracks often appear in the hoof wall. The horse will be unable to retain its shoes, and will become foot sore and lame. This can also happen if a horse's feet have been neglected, inadequately trimmed, or shod infrequently with poor shoeing.

Certain dietary deficiencies will also cause these problems. D.L. Methionine, an amino acid, is often used as a dietary supplement to improve horn growth as it contains sulphur, which is essential for horn production. A deficiency in Biotin, a B vitamin, was thought to be a major cause of poor crumbling horn, and was frequently added to supplements used to promote horn quality.

It takes about 9 months for the hoof wall to grow down from the coronary band to the ground surface. This being the case, any supplements have to be fed for several months in order to observe any change in the quality of the new horn. During this time any other changes in diet, climate and so on, must be taken into consideration when evaluating the possible effects of a supplement on the hoof wall. Dietary changes are reflected in the rings seen on the hoof wall.

Extra calcium can be included in the ration as calcium carbonate (ground limestone), sterilized bone flour, or as calcium lactate or calcium gluconate. The latter two are readily absorbed from the small intestine. Alternately, alfalfa (lucerne), which is high in protein and calcium, can be added to the diet. Bran should be removed from the diet of horses with poor hooves as it is high in phosphorus and ties up the calcium in the food, preventing it being absorbed from the bowel.

LAMINITIS

Laminitis is a common cause of lameness. There are a number of factors which may trigger off an attack of laminitis, the commonest being overfeeding, especially in obese native ponies that are allowed free access to fertilized, lush grassland. Constant trauma due to exercise on hard ground may also precipitate an attack of laminitis. When the feet are neglected, so that the toes become overlong, the laminae are torn apart as the horse walks. If the hoof is over-trimmed or the shoe causes pressure on the sole, laminitis may result.

Laminitis can also be a complication following diseases such as pneumonia, colic and retained afterbirth in the mare. It is also seen in animals which are stressed, and in aged horses with pituitary tumours. Acutely lame horses may develop a weight-bearing laminitis in the opposite limb to the one with the original problem.

By understanding some of the factors which precipitate a laminitic attack, it can be avoided by taking preventive measures.

Signs of Laminitis

Laminitis can occur in all four feet or in any combination of feet. When only the front feet are involved, the horse has a typical camped stance. This is because the hind legs are able to bear more weight when they are placed well under the horse's body, whereas the horse takes more weight on the heels of the front feet when the feet are placed in front of the perpendicular line.

With a case of laminitis the horse may be 'footy' on hard, rough or uneven ground, but may appear sound on softer, smooth ground. Such a horse tends to place the heels on the ground first, so has a classic heel-to-toe gait.

When more than one foot is involved, the horse will constantly shift its weight from one foot to another. It will be reluctant to take extra weight on the most

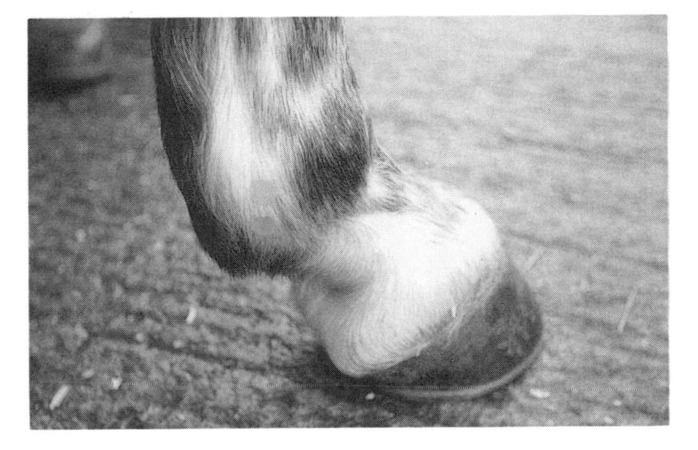

8. The markers show the place where you can feel the digital pulse on the outside (lateral side) of the fetlock joint in a right foreleg.

painful foot and so will object to having the opposite foot picked up.

Although the feet do not always feel hot, there is usually an obvious digital pulse, which can be felt in the arteries that run down the inside and outside of the proximal sesamoids of the fetlock joint.

Laminitis should always be treated as a potentially serious condition and receive prompt veterinary attention.

Treatment

Laminitis is caused by a reduction in the blood flow to the dermal tissues so that the bond between the dermal and epidermal laminae is disrupted. In severe cases the pedal bone either partially separates from the hoof, and the tip penetrates the sole in front of the apex of the frog (*foundered*); or, if all the interlaminar bands are destroyed, the pedal bone becomes detached from the hoof (*a sinker*).

A sinker requires urgent expert veterinary attention if the horse is to survive. A foundered case will need corrective trimming and shoeing if the normal anatomy of the foot is to be restored. Less severe cases usually respond to prompt veterinary treatment with frog supports, painkillers and drugs to reduce blood pressure and improve blood flow to the laminae. All laminitis cases should initially be confined to a stable with a thick, preferably shavings, bed. When the pedal bone is displaced, as in founder or sinker cases, the horse must not be forced to exercise as this would cause further damage to the already unstable hoof/pedal bone.

Most cases are usually x-rayed with markers on the hoof in order to assess the amount of displacement of the pedal bone within the hoof. Sometimes a dorsal wall resection is performed to remove the front wall of the hoof. The horse may be fitted with a special surgical shoe, such as a heart bar shoe, under the supervision of the vet. Nursing is vitally important in cases of laminitis and is very time-consuming.

Owners must be willing to change their management methods radically to prevent further attacks of laminitis if the underlying cause is obesity or overfeeding.

THE FARRIER

All horses, shod or barefoot, will need a farrier at regular intervals. The local veterinary practice or riding establishment will supply the names of registered farriers in the area. Some farriers specialize in surgical shoeing, working closely with the vet in treating foot problems.

All owners require a high standard of work from the farrier, but many expect him to achieve this in dark, dirty conditions on an ill-behaved, unrestrained animal!

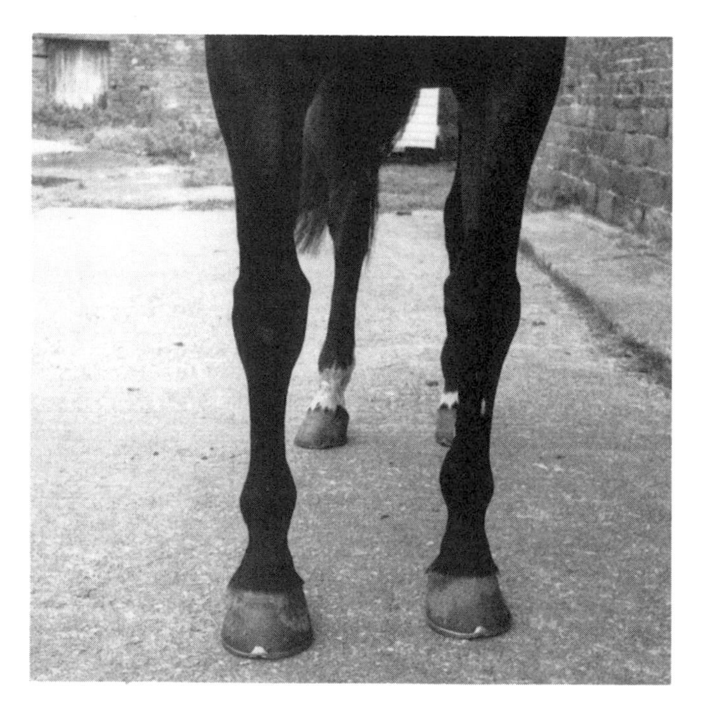

9. The horse should always be presented to the farrier with clean, dry feet and legs.

The horse must be well handled and presented to the farrier with clean feet and legs, preferably in a well-lit stable.

The hoof grows from the coronary band at the rate of 7 mm (¼ in) per month. This means that in the average horse the hoof wall takes 9 months to be replaced. The feet are usually trimmed every 4–6 weeks.

The wall at the heels is continually worn away by friction with the shoe each time the heels expand. The ground surface of the wall at the toe gets little wear in the shod foot. The hoof wall at the toe is older, thicker and more brittle than that of the heels. The farrier will dress the toes well back. Long toes put unnecessary strain on the flexor tendons and the laminae of the dorsal wall. A mechanical laminitis (tearing of the laminae) occurs in over-long toes with the formation of poor-quality, crumbling and frequently infected horn at the white line. This **seedy toe** condition is commonly found in chronic (long-standing) laminitic feet.

After the farrier has dressed the foot and checked that it is balanced, i.e., level from toe to heel and side

Fig. 44. Grooves worn in heels of shoes by friction against the hoof wall during movement

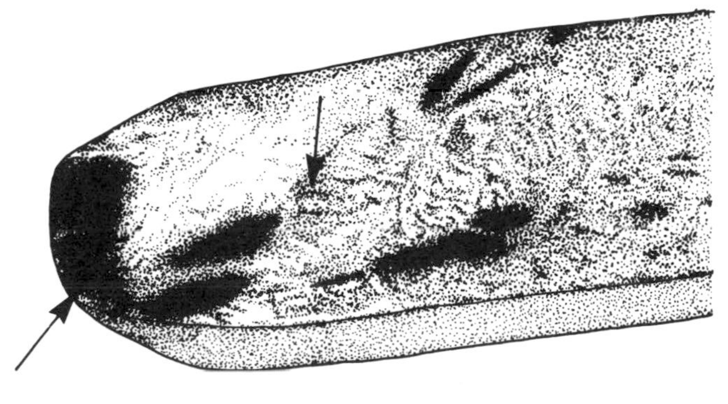

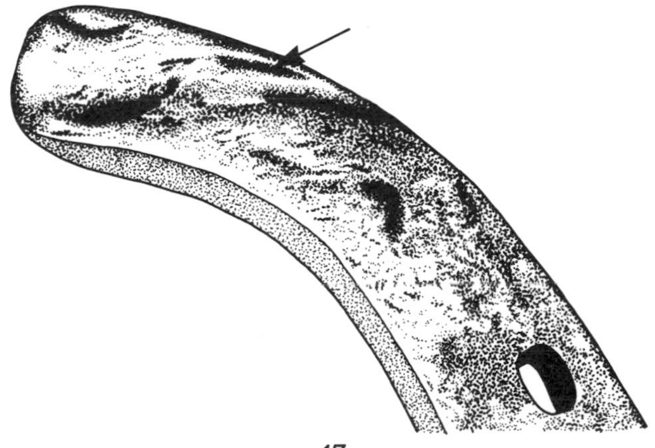

10. Check that the foot is balanced and level. A line straight down from the point of the shoulder should bisect the limb and foot. The ground surface should be parallel to the coronary band.

to side, he will reset the shoe. He may want to walk the horse on a smooth flat surface to make sure the foot is landing flat. If the foot is out of balance because the outside and inside heels do not land together, the heels become *sheared*.

This is commonly caused by one heel being left longer than the other. The longer heel lands first, taking excess weight so the wall becomes straighter and the hair line is pushed upwards. The lower limb joints will be abnormally concussed on that side, which may result in joint disease. The horse will be lame if the heels are completely sheared and most likely develop thrush in the central groove of the frog and between the bulbs of the heels. Special bar shoes are used in cases of sheared heels.

Fig. 45. Sheared heels – the left heel is higher and the wall straighter than the right side

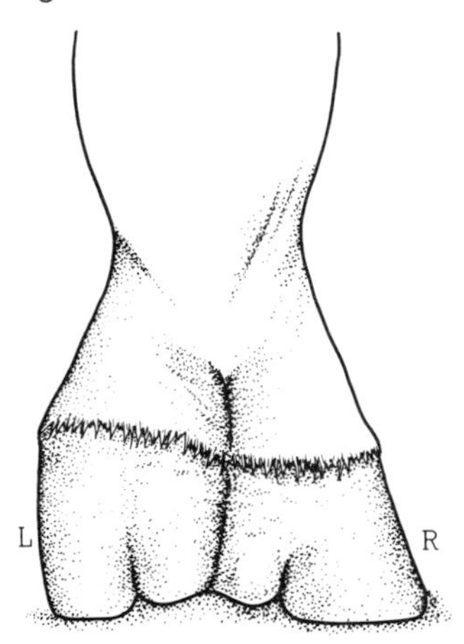

When the metal shoe shows wear, the farrier replaces it with a new machine-made or made-to-measure shoe. They can be applied hot or cold. The nails are placed into the insensitive middle layer of the hoof wall to the outside of the white line. Nails which are too close to the sensitive laminae cause painful pressure, **nail bind**, and if they puncture the sensitive tissue, **nail prick**, can lead to infection.

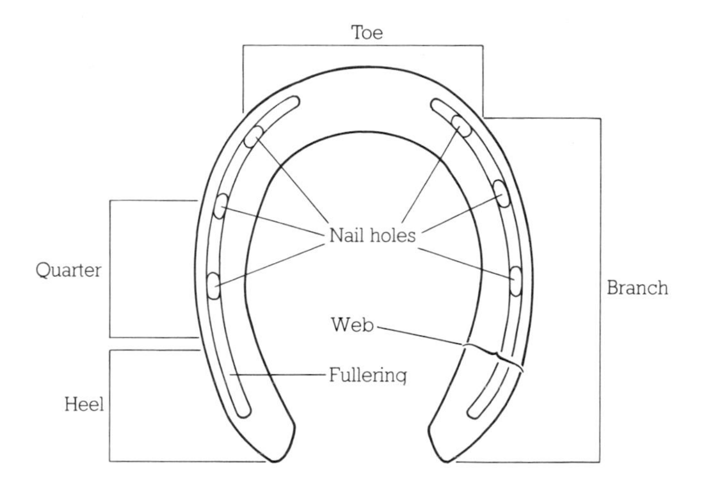

Fig. 46. Ground surface of a horse shoe for a front foot

Nails are not usually placed beyond the curve of the quarters towards the heels.

The shoe sits on the wall of the foot and up to 7 mm (¼ in) onto the sole. The branches should be set wider than the wall from the quarters to the heel to allow for foot expansion. The shoe should go beyond the heels to give good support to the heels. Shoes which are too short cause heels to become underrun and collapse, and may predispose to navicular disease. By shoeing wide and long it is possible to spread a narrow foot and open out contracted heels.

When all the shoes have been reset the farrier will trot the horse up to make sure it is not lame due to a tight shoe, nail bind or nail prick. This is the time to make arrangements for your next appointment with the farrier – do not wait until the shoes are falling off!

CHECKLIST – FOOTCARE

1 Check normal stance and gait.

2 Pick out feet daily: check for heat, pain, smell, injuries, foreign bodies.

3 Apply hoof dressing if necessary.

4 Note shoe position and wear; raised clenches.

5 Make appointment with farrier every 4–6 weeks.

6 AFTER shoeing, Trot up
Check length/width of branches;
foot/pastern angle; foot balance.

CHAPTER 6
SKIN CARE

STRUCTURE OF THE SKIN

The skin is the protective covering of the body, and the largest organ. It consists of a superficial layer, the *epidermis*, a stratified epithelium, and a deeper layer, the *dermis* or *corium*, which is dense connective tissue. The dermis is separated from the underlying tissue by a layer of subcutaneous tissue. This is a loose connective tissue containing elastic fibres, muscle fibres and fat deposits. The subcutaneous tissue allows

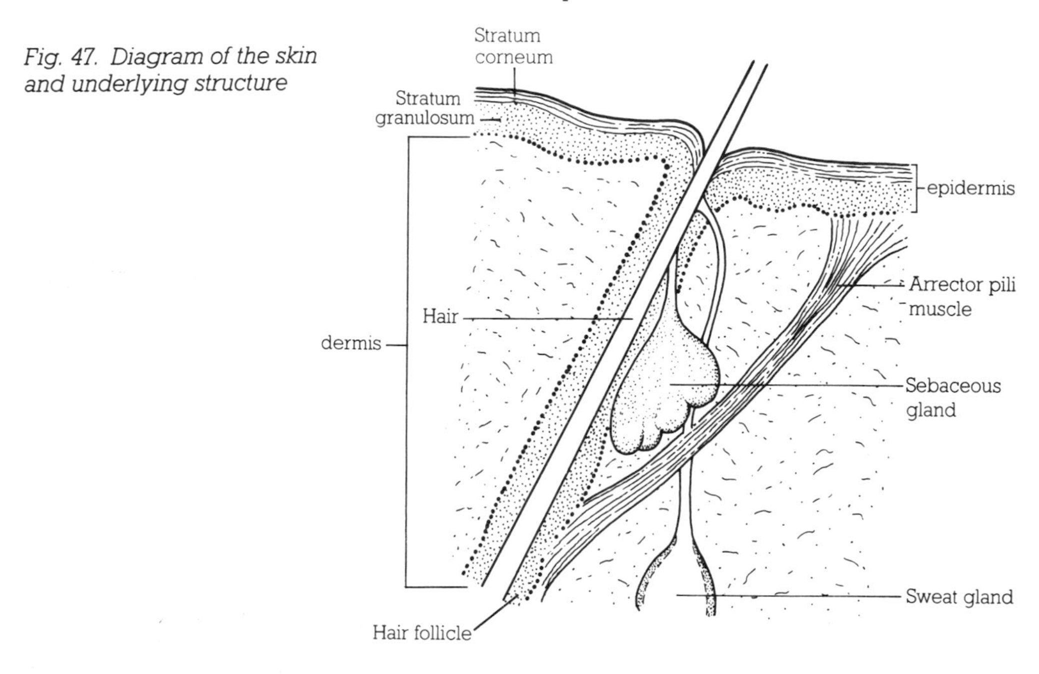

Fig. 47. Diagram of the skin and underlying structure

the skin to move over the underlying tissue.

The thickness of the skin varies in different parts of the body from 1–5 mm. The skin is thickest at the base of the mane and on the upper surface of the tail.

The deepest layer of the epidermis has columnar-shaped cells, while those nearer the surface are flatter and become harder and drier until they eventually die and flake off as dandruff or scurf. The rate of cell production in the deeper layers is affected by increased blood supply and constant friction. This is seen in sites of chronic inflammation and areas of callus formation where the epidermis is much thicker.

The dermis is divided into a papillary layer below the epidermis and a deeper reticular layer. It is well supplied with blood vessels, nerves, sweat glands, sebaceous glands and hair follicles. The hair follicles are formed as a thickening and indentation of the epidermis into the dermis. This also forms the sebaceous gland associated with the hair follicle.

Most of the body is covered in hair and even those parts which initially appear bare have sparse, fine hair. Each hair goes through a growth cycle with a resting stage and a growing stage. Hair is continually falling out and being replaced.

In the spring and autumn, large numbers of hairs are shed over a short period of time when the horse changes its coat type. The summer coat being finer and shorter than the long, thick winter coat.

The hair protects the skin from ultraviolet light, heat and cold, promotes evaporation of sweat and water, and aids the excretion of certain minerals such as copper, lead and arsenic. In certain areas there are special hairs, such as long tactile hairs on the muzzle,

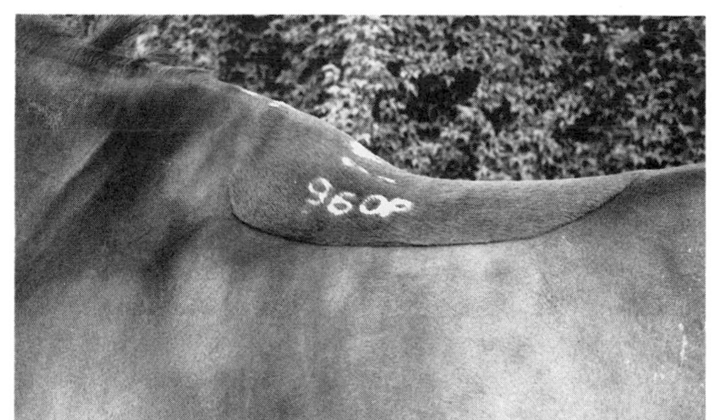

11. The thicker winter coat has been clipped off this hunter, except for the saddle patch, which shows a freeze brand.

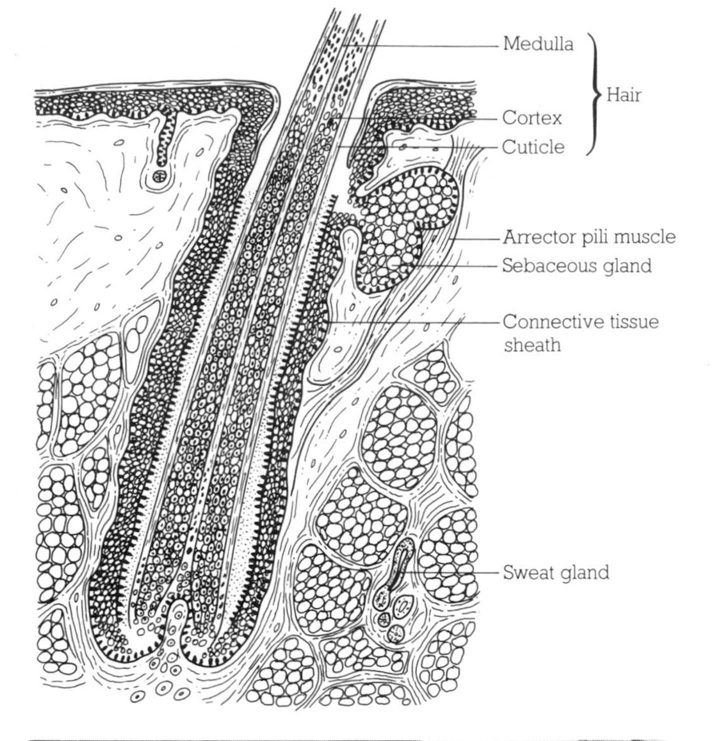

Fig. 48. Structure of hair shaft and associated glands

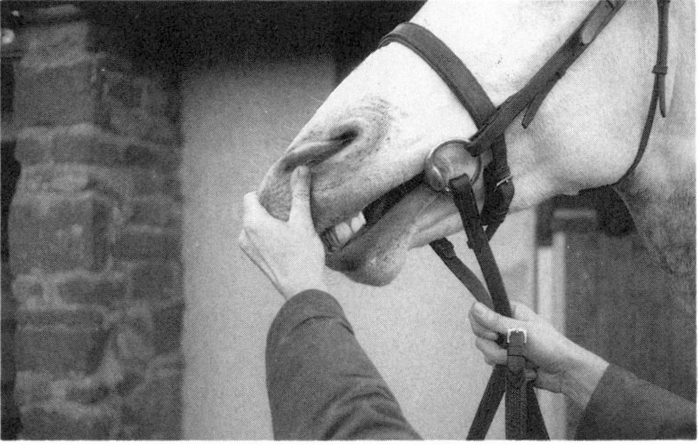

12. Long tactile hairs can be seen around the chin and muzzle on this 7-year-old mare.

nostrils, the ears and the eyelashes. These hairs play a role as sensory organs. They are surrounded by nerves that react to pressure on the hair shaft. The hairs of the mane and tail and the feathering on the flexor surface of the fetlock are especially long and coarser than body hair.

The hair is divided into a shaft, above the skin surface, and a root and rounded bulb which are in the hair follicle. The hair consists of an inner medulla and an outer cortex covered by a thin horny cuticle.

The medulla is a soft core with air spaces and a few pigment cells (*melanocytes*). This gives a silver or white colour to the hair if the cortex contains no pigment.

The cortex has several layers of cornified cells. The amount and type of pigment (*melanin*) within these cells determines hair colour, either black, brown or red. Scattered smooth clusters of melanin granules in the cortex produce light chestnut hair. Densely packed, large, irregular clusters produce black hair. Variations between these extremes give the other coat colours, e.g., mahogany bay, brown and liver chestnut. Duns have a greater amount of pigment on one side of the hair shaft than the other. Greys have a mixture of black and white hairs; usually the number of white hairs increase with age.

All colours except albinos (creams) have pigmented skin. Unpigmented skin is more susceptible to the effects of sunlight and may develop sunburn. It is also more likely to become affected by photosensitivity especially after eating plants containing photodynamic substances such as St Johns wort.

The pigmentation of the hoof wall corresponds to the hair colour at the coronary band. Black hooves are stronger than unpigmented hooves.

Sebaceous glands secrete a fatty substance that waterproofs and oils the skin and hair. Contraction of the muscle which straightens the hair assists in emptying the gland into the hair follicle. The glands of the lips, mammary gland, prepuce and perineum and those of the ear canal and eyelids empty directly onto the skin surface.

Sweat glands are well developed in most areas of the skin in the horse. The greatest numbers and the largest being at the sides of the nostrils, the flank and the mammary gland. The sweat gland consists of a long tube which ends in a coiled mass in the dermis. It opens either into a hair follicle in the epidermis or by a funnel-shaped pore onto the skin surface. They are essential in temperature regulation and electrolyte (salt) balance.

The chestnuts and ergots are keratinized or cornified epithelium. The chestnuts are thought to be the vestige of the first digit. They are horn-like structures on the inside of the horse's legs. They are found above the knee on the inside of the fore-arm and on the inside of the hock. They are unique to each horse and can be used to identify a particular animal, like finger prints in humans.

The ergots are small projections of cornified tissue in the centre of the flexor surface of the fetlock. They are often hidden by a tuft of hair or feathering in heavy horses. Ergots may be the vestiges of the second and fifth digit of extinct forms of the horse.

GROOMING

Horses in their natural surroundings keep their skin and coat in good order by rubbing, scratching, shaking, licking, nibbling and rolling. These activities remove dirt, debris, scurf and parasites from the skin and hair.

They clean their eyes, face and nose by rubbing their face up and down a foreleg or on an inanimate object. Horses snort to clean out their nostrils. The neck and crest are groomed by rubbing them up and down on objects such as trees and fences or on the ground when rolling. The buttocks and tail head are also rubbed on posts and trees to clean the underside of the tail of grease and faecal contamination (as the tail is pushed across the opposing skin). Excessive rubbing of the crest and tail can damage the hair and break the skin surface as well as wrecking fences and gates. This is seen in animals with sweetitch (see page 57) and lice infestation (see page 57).

Mutual grooming is also practised between horses; they face each other and nibble their companion's withers.

There are several factors that may make self-grooming difficult for a horse. Horses roaming free rarely lie down on areas contaminated by faeces, but stabled horses may have no choice, so become covered in stable stains. A stabled horse may not have adequate space to roll or it may wear a rug, which makes self-grooming difficult. When horses are ill they spend less time on self-grooming or stop altogether, so the coat becomes neglected, dirty, harsh and staring.

Normally, horses should be groomed every day. Grooming not only keeps the coat and skin clean, it aids in the dispersal of oil from the sebaceous glands, it helps remove parasites and it massages the skin. It is also an ideal time to examine the horse for signs of injury and skin diseases. It is important not to be heavy-handed when brushing the sensitive areas like the head and inner thigh, and boney parts such as the hocks and elbows.

One sponge should be used to wipe around the eyes and nostrils and another for the dock and surrounding area. Discharges from the eyes and nose may be the first sign of a respiratory infection. When washing the dock of a mare it is often possible to detect if she is in season. The dock is a common site for the melanoma tumour.

Horses which are permanently kept at grass are normally only groomed with a dandy brush or rubber curry comb to remove mud and dirt prior to exercise. The grease is left on the coat to waterproof it, so the body brush is not used. The tail and mane are kept free of tangles, burrs and twigs and the tail is trimmed so that it does not trail along muddy ground.

In windy, wet weather horses stop grazing and turn their hindquarters into the wind. They clamp their tails between their hind legs so that the tail hair shields the hairless inguinal region and inner thigh. This prevents heat loss and conserves energy. If the tail is pulled and thinned this protective function of the tail is lost. It is wiser to leave grass-kept horses with full manes and tails in the winter. The tail also acts as a fly switch in the summer.

The daily routine should always include picking out the feet.

Horses without access to shelter or shade may suffer from sunburn, especially on unpigmented areas of skin such as the flesh marks on the muzzle. These can be protected by a high-factor sun cream designed for babies. Horses eating certain plants, such as St Johns wort, and those with liver disease, are susceptible to photosensitization. Shade is also necessary to prevent the horses being worried by flies.

FLIES

A number of species of flies cause problems, e.g., fly worry, restlessness, painful bites and skin diseases, to the horse.

The *Musca* species feed around the eyelids, which causes excessive tear formation with overflow down the face. This results in an ulcerative dermatitis which attracts more flies. A fly fringe is a useful preventive measure. This species will feed on wounds and any discharges from the nostrils, etc., causing further skin damage. Flies may lay eggs in neglected wounds, and developing maggots cause extensive tissue damage (*fly strike*).

The horse may be worried by small black flies (*Simulium* species) which bite the ears, causing it to rub and shake its head. Some horses develop thick white plaques on the inside of the ear as a reaction to these bites. Mesh hoods and fly repellents are commonly used to control this problem. Mange mites may also cause head shaking and lesions in the ears.

CHECKLIST – SIGNS OF SKIN DISEASE

1	Loss of hair	→	Bald areas		
2	Itchy	→	Rubbing	→	Self-inflicted skin injury
3	Abnormal behaviour	→	Restless, head-tossing Stamping feet, irritable		
4	Hair reaction	→	Dull, scurfy coat, broken hair		
5	Skin reaction	→	Scabs, pustules, raised wheals, ulcers, wounds		

The stable fly, *Stomoxys cacitrans*, may annoy the horse and give painful bites, as well as transmitting blood-borne diseases. Some horses are hypersensitive to fly bites and develop large, raised swellings with a scab in the centre at the site of the bite. These are often painful and itchy.

Summer sheets or fly sheets and hoods can be worn to protect the horse from fly bites, and stable walls can be treated with insecticidal solutions, or insecticidal strips can be hung in the stable. Manure and compost heaps, a breeding ground for flies, should not be situated near the stable and should be sprayed with insecticides.

Adult bot flies (*Gasterophilus* species) lay small yellow eggs on the hairs of the legs and lower body of the horse. These eggs must be removed with a special comb or safety razor to prevent the horse ingesting them. Fly repellents can be applied to the horse to prevent the egg-laying.

Some horses and ponies are allergic to the bites of the *Culicoides* species of midge. The intense irritation (*pruritis*) causes them to rub incessantly at their necks, withers and tails. This damages the hair and skin, causing loss of mane and tail and eventual thickening of the skin along the crest and tail head.

Once a horse is sensitized to midge bites, it will suffer from **sweetitch** (recurring seasonal dermatitis) each year unless preventive measures are used. Depending on the weather conditions the midges are active from April to October. They are prevalent near water, under trees, around manure heaps and on low-lying marshy ground. They are seen in large numbers on muggy days. They feed on the horse in the early evening until dark.

Susceptible animals should be stabled from mid afternoon. Make sure that the stable door and window are made insect-proof with mosquito netting or fine net-curtain material. Spray the stable walls with insecticidal solutions, and hang insecticidal strips from the ceiling.

Cover the horse regularly in fly repellent or mineral oil containing an insecticide to prevent the midges from biting. Hoods and rugs are useful in keeping the midges at bay.

Although long-acting corticosteroid injections do alleviate the irritation and so stop the horse rubbing, they are not to be recommended because of the serious side effects, including laminitis. Sweetitch can be successfully controlled by careful management, so there is no need to resort to these injections.

There are numerous fly repellents and insecticides on the market. They should always be used in accordance with the manufacturers' directions. When using a product for the first time it is advisable to 'test dose' it on a small area of skin rather than cover the whole body, just in case the horse has an adverse reaction to the drug. Any abnormal reaction, should be immediately reported to the veterinary supplier and the manufacturers.

LICE

Horses that are itchy and rub their head, neck and flanks in the winter time, producing large areas of hair loss, are frequently infested with **lice**. If the horse has a dull, scaley coat with a moth-eaten appearance, lice infestation should be suspected. Heavy infestations with lice are very debilitating and the horse may become anaemic and susceptible to other infections.

There are two types of lice – biting and sucking. On careful examination the lice and their eggs (nits) can be seen on the hair and skin. Lice are cigar shaped, creamish yellow to light brown in colour and 2–3 mm in length.

Dusting powder and washes containing organo-phosphorus compounds or permethrin are commonly used to kill the parasites. If the horse has a very thick coat it is impossible for a powder to reach the skin, so a wash may be more effective. Obviously as this is a winter and early spring complaint, it is not an ideal time of year to wash a horse, especially if it is in a weak condition and therefore more prone to chilling. The thick coat may have to be clipped off so the horse can be treated and then rugged up. All brushes and rugs and in-contact horses should also be treated.

Fig. 49. a) Biting louse

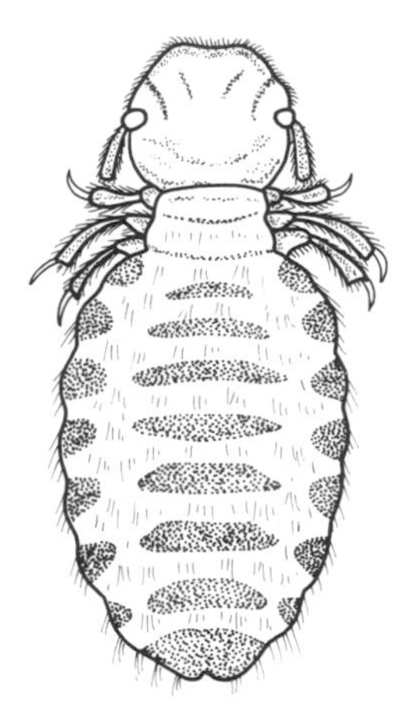

b) sucking louse

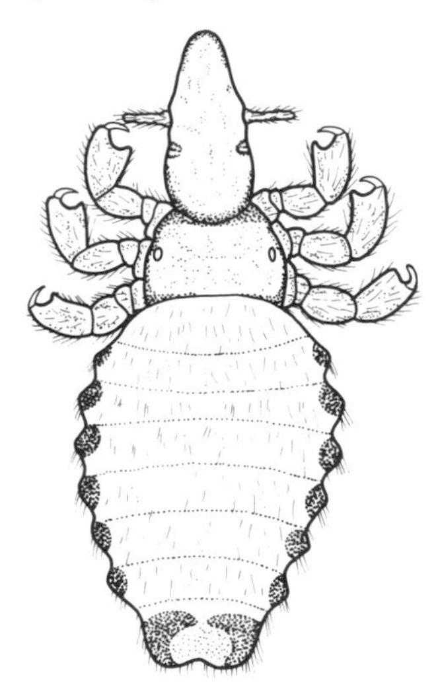

OTHER SKIN COMPLAINTS

Horses with small bald areas which are not pruritic may have **ringworm**, which will require diagnosis and treatment by a vet.

Horses with itchy legs and lower body may have a **mange** infection. This can be complicated with 'greasy

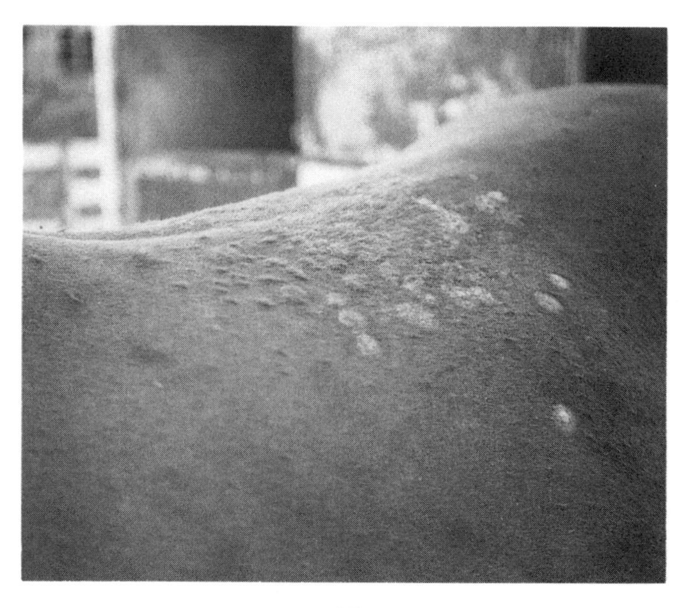

13. Ringworm lesions on a horse's back.

heel', especially in horses with a lot of feather.

Another common autumn/winter skin condition is caused by the organism *Dermatophilus congolensis.* This type of organism is responsible for two conditions in the horse, **rainscald** and **mud fever**. The organism penetrates wet skin, causing exudative dermatitis (serum oozes from the inflamed skin). These conditions are seen when it is very wet and muddy underfoot, and during times of persistent heavy rainfall. Rainscald lesions appear on the neck, shoulders, back and rump of affected animals. The skin will be covered in crusty scabs, large areas may be matted together and the hair often sticks up in tufts giving a paint-brush effect.

Mud rash is seen on the legs, especially the back of the pastern; the heels may also be cracked. The limb is often hot, swollen and painful to touch and the horse may be lame. There is often a secondary bacterial infection that requires antibiotic therapy.

These conditions occur in horses which are continually wet and the skin has no chance of drying off.

The obvious method of control is to stable the horse in wet weather, making sure that the bed is dry. A New Zealand rug will keep the horse's body dry and a waterproof barrier cream can be applied to dry, clean legs prior to turning out or exercising. If possible, horses should be grazed on well-drained fields in winter time. If hay is fed on the field, it should be put on the highest land to keep mud to the minimum.

When grooming, it is important to examine the horse carefully for signs of skin disease. As with most diseases, if they are detected early and treated promptly, the treatment is easier, less time-consuming and less expensive, and the recovery time is quicker.

WASHING THE HORSE

Horses are washed to remove dirt from the hair and skin, not as an alternative to grooming. Using recommended horse shampoo in warm water, lather the shampoo into the coat and then thoroughly rinse it out. Use a sweat scraper to remove the excess water, then rug up or walk the horse until it is dry to prevent chilling. If there is no urgency to wash the horse it is best to wait for a warm day. Frequent washing removes all the oil from the coat and skin, and changes the natural acidity of the skin surface.

Fly repellents have to be re-applied after the horse has been washed.

Washing the Sheath

When a stallion or gelding stales (urinates) the penis comes out of the sheath and can be visually examined. If the penis is dirty, i.e., covered with flakes of dead skin and black greasy material (smegma) then it and the sheath will require washing. Often the smegma accumulates into 'beans' in the fold of the penis above the opening of the urethra (the tube which carries urine from the bladder to the exterior). These hard 'beans' cause irritation and can block the urethral opening, making urination difficult. Sometimes horses with dirty sheaths kick at their abdomens and rub their tails because of the discomfort.

The smegma has an unpleasant odour so it is advisable to wear disposable rubber gloves when washing out the sheath, otherwise the smell clings to the hands. Use lukewarm water and a mild soap on pieces of cotton wool to clean out the sheath and penis. Restrain the horse and carry out the procedure in a quiet and gentle manner so that he doesn't object to it on the next occasion. All the soap must be thoroughly rinsed away to prevent any irritation. Frequent washing and vigorous scrubbing will cause more harm than good and encourage excess smegma production. The end of the penis should be examined for any kind of tumour (growth) development as this is a common site for the malignant squamous cell carcinoma, which needs early detection if treatment is to be successful.

Washing the Udder

Mares sometimes have a greasy black accumulation of dirt and skin debris between the two halves of the udder. This should be carefully washed away with warm soapy water, rinsed thoroughly and the udder carefully dried. Some mares are quite ticklish, so the handler must restrain them adequately so that no one is kicked.

The udder and teats can be examined at the same time as washing them for any hard lumps or painful swellings, e.g., **mastitis** (inflammation of the udder due to a bacterial infection).

CLIPPING

Horses need to be clipped only if they are in regular heavy work, which causes their thick coats to become soaked in sweat and difficult to dry.

The horse should be clean and dry prior to clipping. The clippers must be well serviced with sharp blades. All electrical plugs, cables and extension leads must be safe and not positioned where the horse can step on them. If the horse is being clipped for the first time, arrange for an experienced person to do it and choose an easy, quick clip. Clippers should be thoroughly cleaned and disinfected between horses to prevent the spread of skin diseases. They can be sprayed with a fungicidal solution if there is any suspicion of ringworm infection. Some horses object to electric clippers, in which case hand-held mechanical clippers can be used instead. Sedating the horse for clipping has variable results and is not always a reliable way of controlling it.

After the horse is clipped, it will require rugging up in the stable and when grazing. Exercise sheets and blankets may also be needed to prevent the horse being stressed by cold weather. If the legs are clipped out, stable bandages should be used to keep the legs warm. The hair under the saddle (saddle patch) should be left on to prevent the saddle rubbing the skin and causing a sore back.

WASHING GROOMING KITS, RUGS, NUMNAHS

It is important to clean the grooming kit regularly to remove dirt and grease, as well as killing any fungi, bacteria or external parasites that may be on the brushes and cause skin diseases. Each horse should have its own grooming kit so that skin diseases such as ringworm are not so readily transmitted from one animal to another. If a horse is being treated for a particular disease, all the in-contact tack, brushes, rugs, numnahs, etc., should also be washed in the same drug at the same time. This will prevent the horse becoming re-infected.

Biological detergents and disinfectants should not be used on rugs, girths and numnahs unless they can be thoroughly rinsed off. Numerous horses develop **contact allergies** to these substances. Some horses even show contact allergies, on the skin over the rib cage behind the girth, to the rider's rubber riding boots.

RUGS AND BLANKETS

Rugs and blankets must fit properly and be fixed in position by rollers, padded surcingles, or cross-over surcingles and leg straps. Badly fitting rugs cause friction injuries to the skin, and these are commonly seen on the shoulders, brisket and withers.

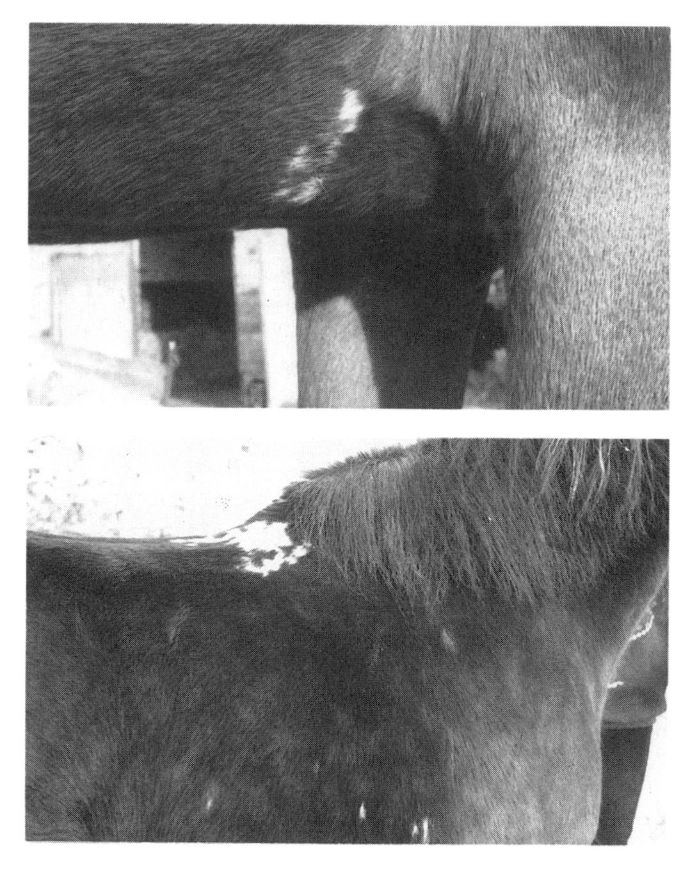

14. Acquired marks on the girth can be caused by a badly fitting or dirty girth.

15. Acquired marks on the withers caused by a badly fitting saddle or roller.

Damage to the skin results in loss of pigment and white hair. These acquired marks on the withers and saddle patches are often caused by rollers and badly fitting saddles.

Rugs must always be checked to make sure they will stay in position whatever the horse does. They can cause horrific accidents if they partly fall off, catching the horse's limbs.

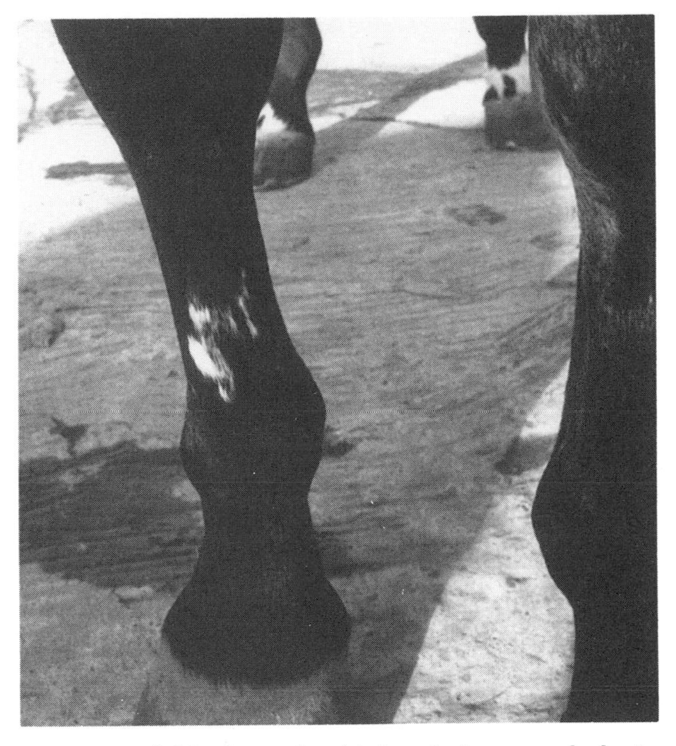

16. Acquired marks on the front of the cannon bone can be caused by incorrect bandaging.

Rugs and blankets should be shaken regularly to remove bedding, hair and dirt, and left out to air. They can be washed in a pure soap-powder or as recommended by the manufacturer. Dry cleaning chemicals may cause a skin reaction in some horses, so should not be used. Blankets and rugs used on sick animals or those with skin diseases must be disinfected before using on another horse.

TACK

A number of skin injuries occur as a direct consequence of poorly fitting tack, e.g., saddle sores and girth galls. Reputable saddlers will always assist in tack-fitting and it is worth seeking their advice. Some horses, because of their conformation, are difficult to fit with a saddle. Narrow horses with high withers and fat horses with ill-defined withers are especially awkward to find a saddle for which does not move about or injure the back. If a horse is purchased in a very fat or thin condition, it is best not to buy a saddle until the animal is at the correct body-weight and its shape is constant.

A saddle which is a poor fit will move about, causing friction on the hair and skin. The hair will become ruffled and break off. There may be bald patches and the skin may be hot and painful to the touch, and raised in a wheal. If this is neglected, the area will take a considerable time to heal. Each time the saddle is removed, the back and girth should be checked for the first signs of friction and pressure sores.

A damaged saddle with a broken or twisted tree will give the horse a sore back. If the saddle needs re-flocking (stuffing) or the stuffing is lumpy, this will cause the horse discomfort. Riding with a loose girth also allows the saddle to move about too much.

The rider may also contribute to pressure sores on the horse's back by not sitting correctly in the saddle. If the rider sits to one side, putting more weight on one seat bone, this tends to twist the saddle and put uneven stress on the horse's back.

Horses with sore backs should not be ridden until the lesion has healed. They may be exercised on a lunge instead.

Sometimes the horse has skin nodules under the saddle area, these may be caused by warbles or nodular skin disease. A thick sponge with holes cut in it to correspond with the position of the nodules will remove any pressure and prevent them ulcerating. The alternative is to have any troublesome nodules surgically removed.

Thick sheepskin numnahs are useful for thin-skinned horses in poor condition to avoid rubs from the saddle. Sheepskin sleeves can also be fitted over the girth to prevent galling. Dirty girths are a common cause of girth galls. All tack should be supple and clean. Numnahs and girth sleeves must be washed frequently in a mild soap. Exercise boots should be kept scrupulously clean to prevent rubs on the legs.

Head-shaking is sometimes caused by the pain and discomfort of badly fitting tack. Any horse fidgeting with its mouth or head should have the tack, especially the bit, and its mouth, including teeth, checked. Bits which are too small, too big or too thin, or in the wrong position in the mouth, may cause problems. Injuries to the corners of the mouth may be caused by an incorrectly fitted bit or a heavy-handed rider. If the cause of these injuries is not discovered, they are unlikely to heal and the condition will recur.

Make sure you choose a pony or horse which is the correct size and temperament for the rider.

Taking a horse's body temperature using a stubby bulb clinical thermometer.

Trotting the horse towards the vet to detect foreleg lameness.

Exercising on a lunge.

This horse has lost its lower incisors, resulting in the upper incisors becoming over-long due to lack of wear.

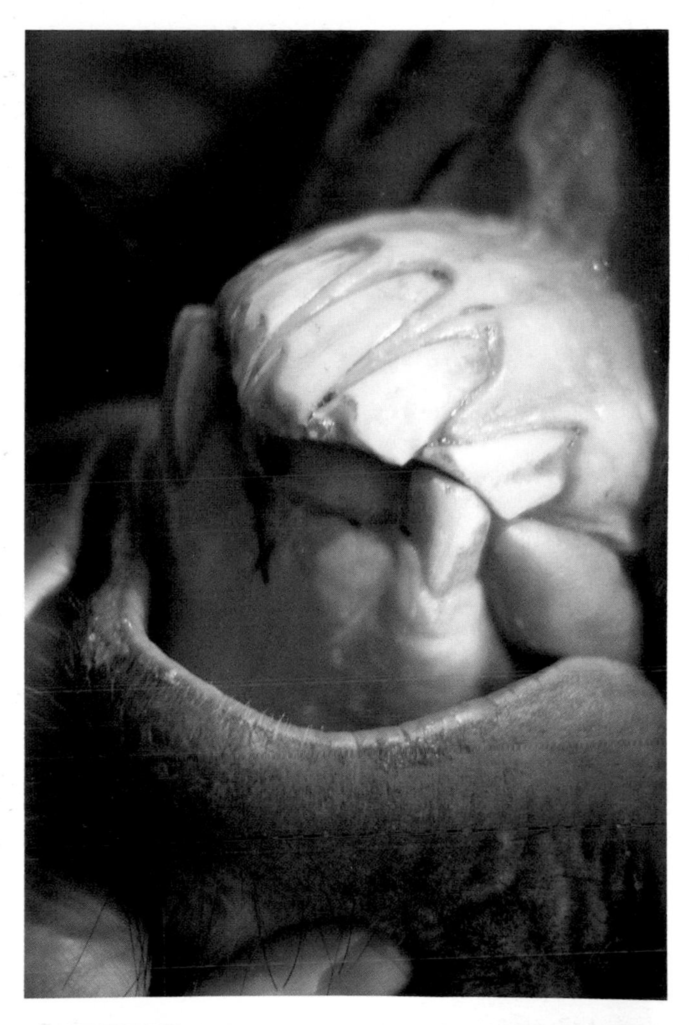

Foundered foot fitted with a heart-bar shoe. This type of shoe has a special v-shaped bar which is carefully fitted over the frog. X-rays are used to calculate the exact length of bar required.

Measuring the height of a pony. The handler covers the pony's eye so it cannot see the measuring stick and take fright.

Condition scoring viewing from the side. This pony has a condition score of 3.

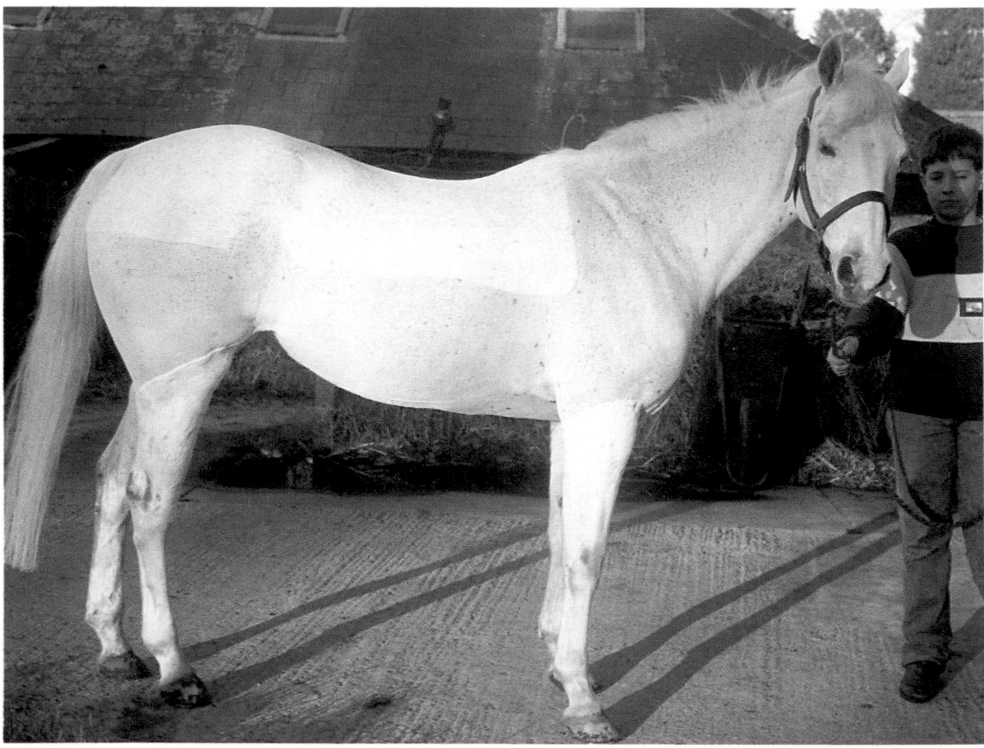

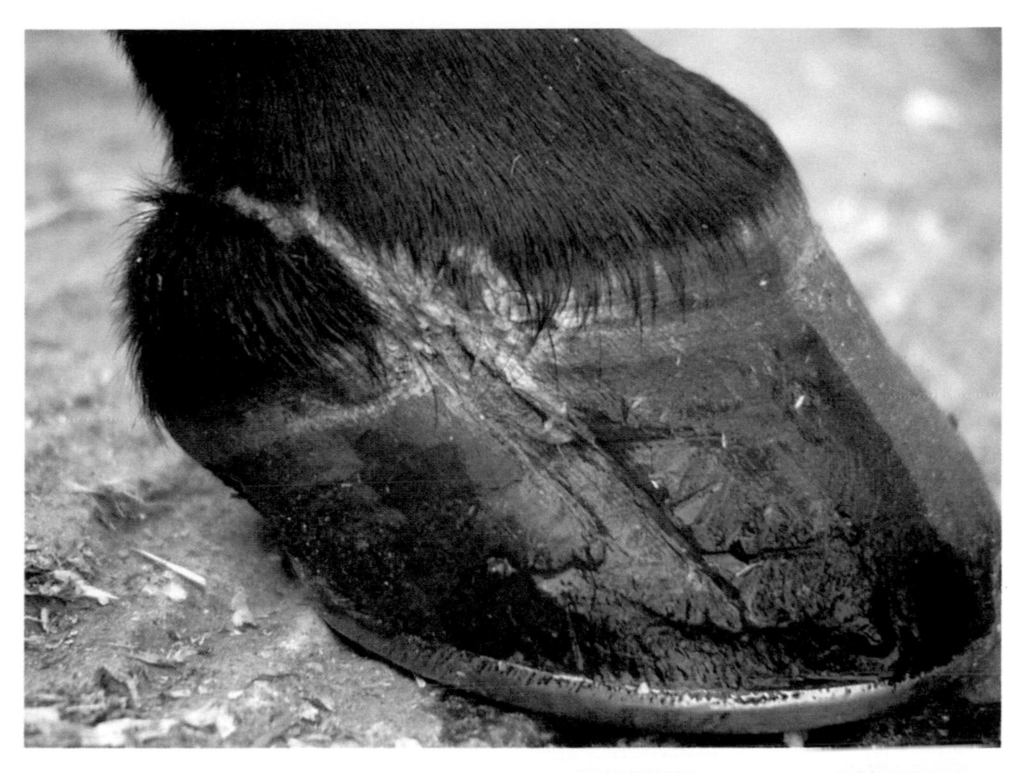

An injury to the heel, which involved the coronary band, has caused a defect in the wall horn at the quarter.

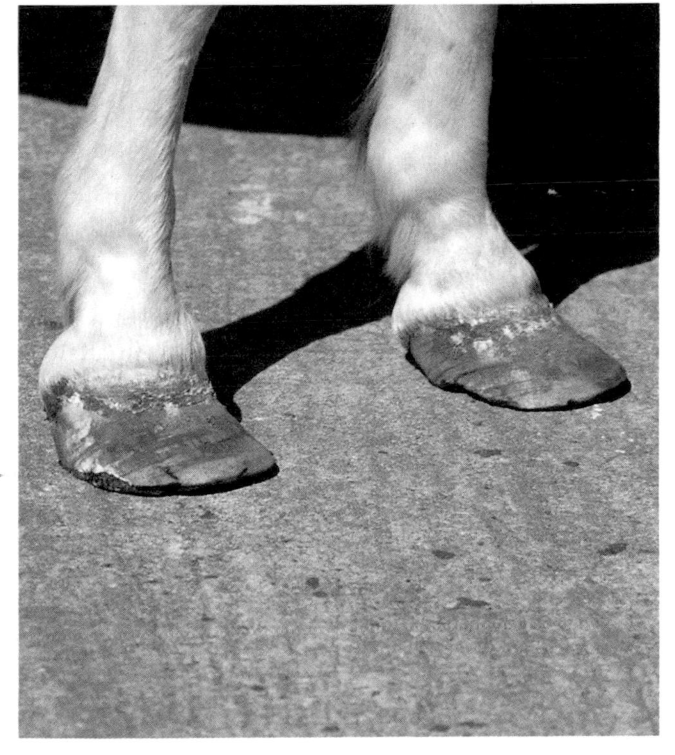

Over-long feet in this animal caused laminitis. The horse's weight is on the heels of the front feet. As it walks the laminae at the toe are torn apart.

A special plastic glue-on shoe with an adjustable heart-bar. This type of shoe is used to treat laminitis.

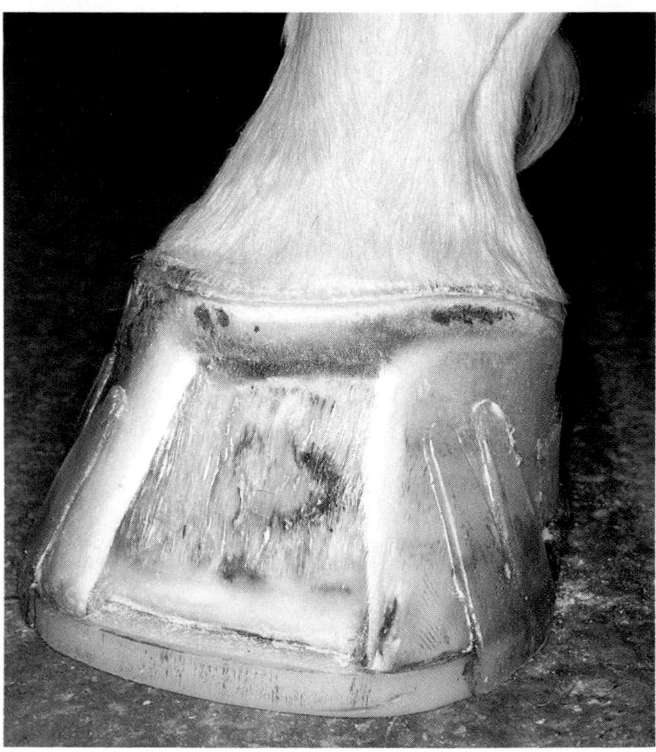

Dorsal wall resection on the right fore, fitted with a glue-on heart-bar shoe.

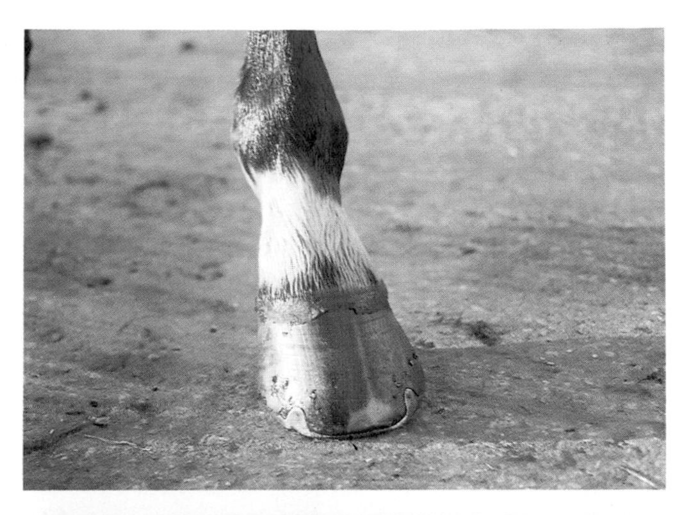

The colour of the hoof wall corresponds to the hair colour at the coronary band. This is used to describe the horse in identification documents and vaccination certificates.

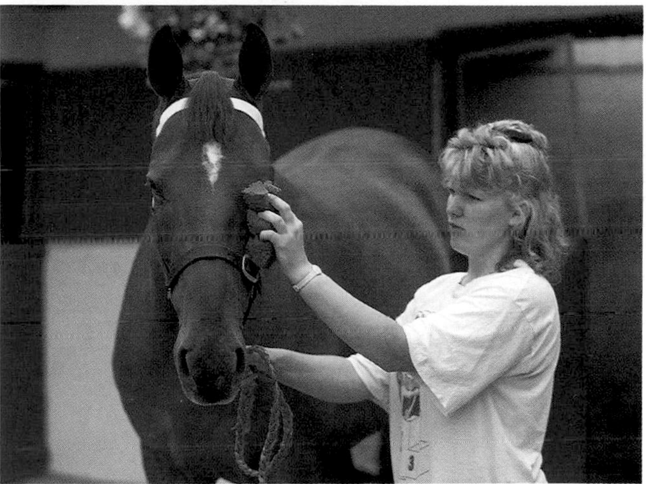

Using a clean damp sponge any discharges are carefully removed from around the eyes.

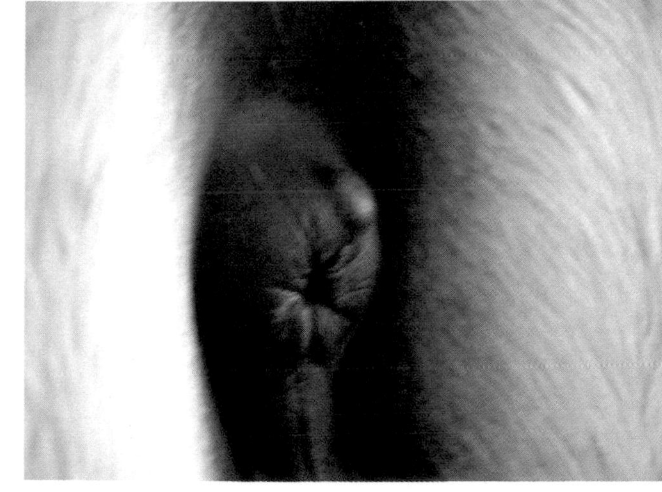

Melanoma are commonly seen under the dock area. Here is one to the top right of the anus.

This mare has developed an allergic reaction on her head to fly bites. The whole head is covered in raised plaques (urticaria).

Pony fitted with a New Zealand rug.

Horses with abdominal pain (colic) will often roll excessively.

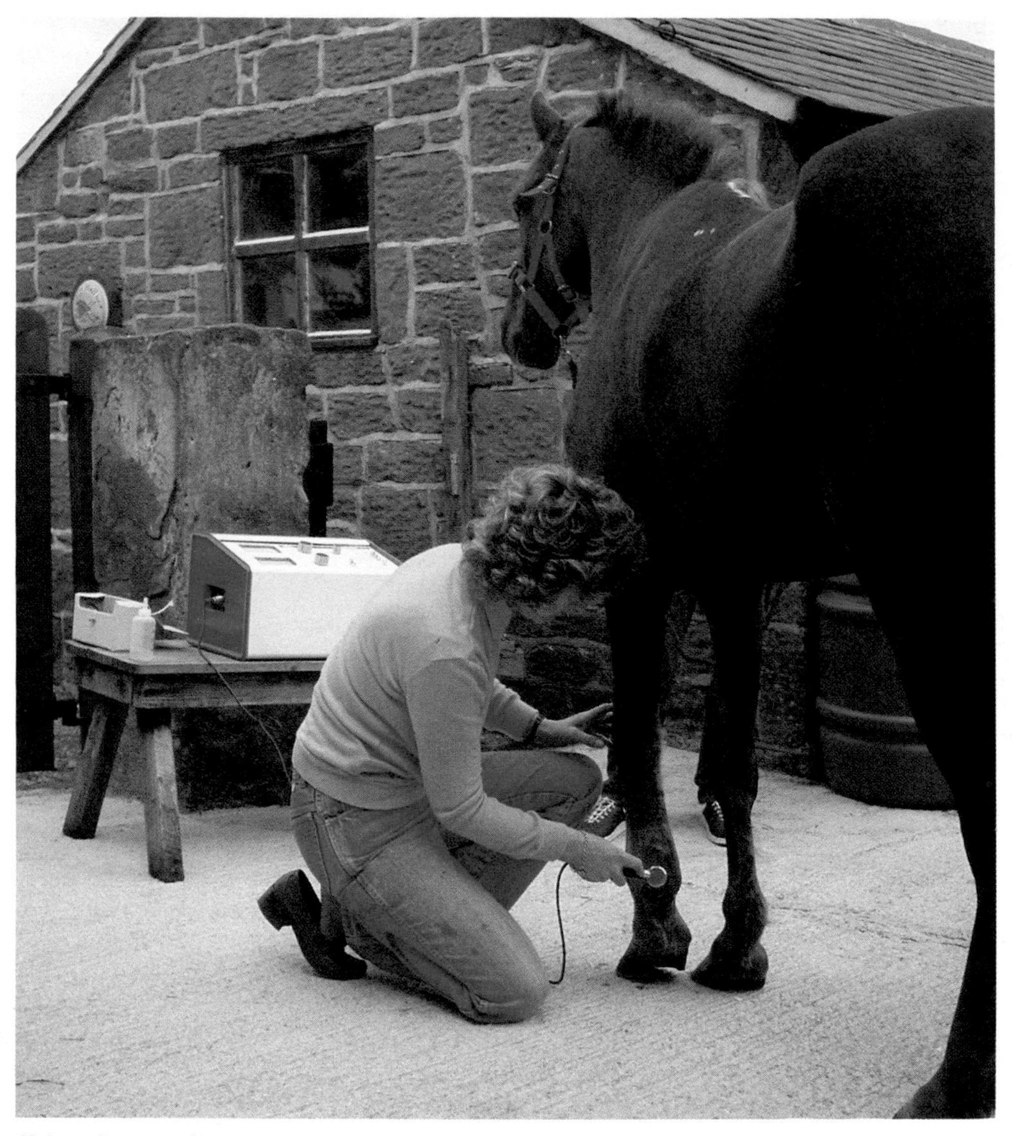

Using ultrasound massage on a sprained fetlock to reduce swelling.

An 18-year-old pony showing Galvayne's groove running down the middle of the corner incisor.

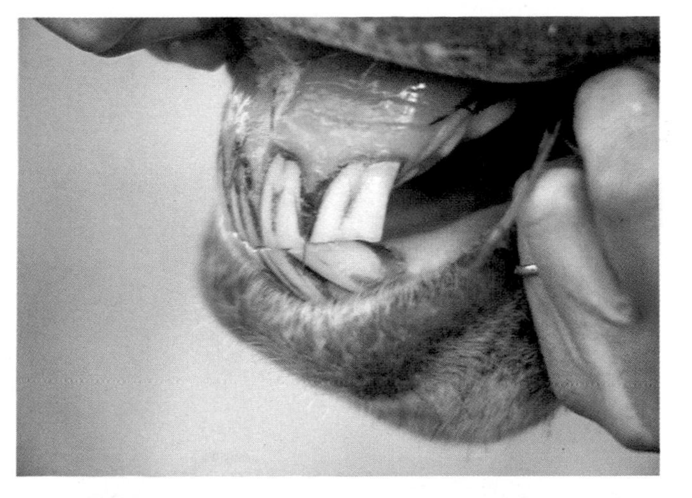

Red dots show the position of the facial artery where it is possible to feel a pulse.

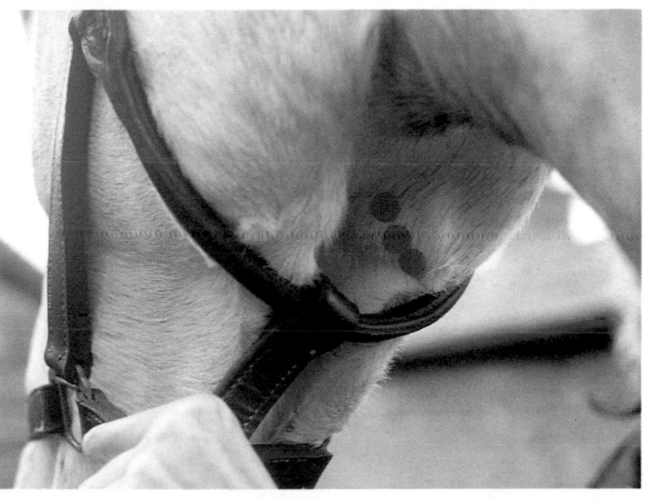

Holding a horse in order to examine the right dental arcades for rasping.

This stable is large, airy and well lit. The doorway is wide so that the horse does not injure itself going in or out of the stable.

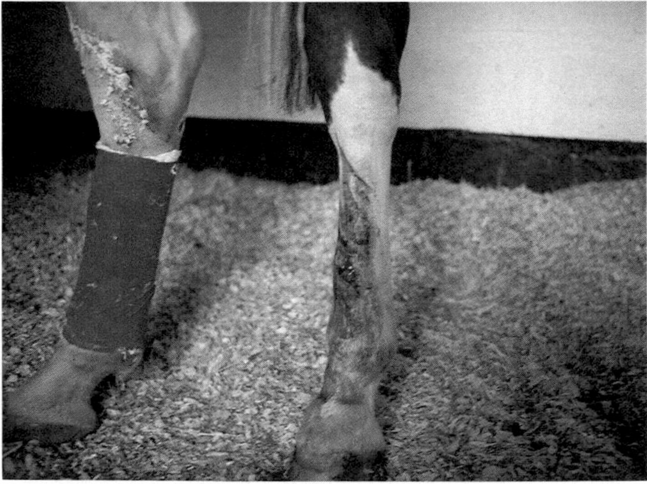

Barbed-wire injuries to the hind legs.

Horse and rider must be clearly visible to other road-users.

A horse dressed in protective clothing for travelling in a horse box.

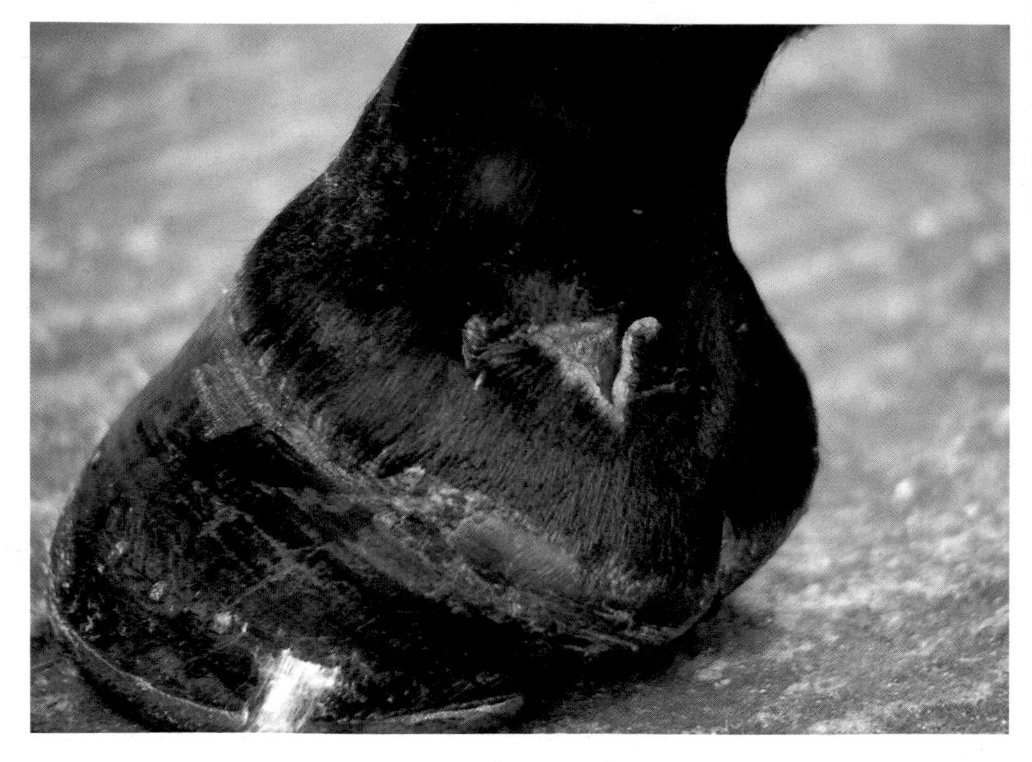

A jagged, full-thickness skin wound on the lateral bulb of the heel.

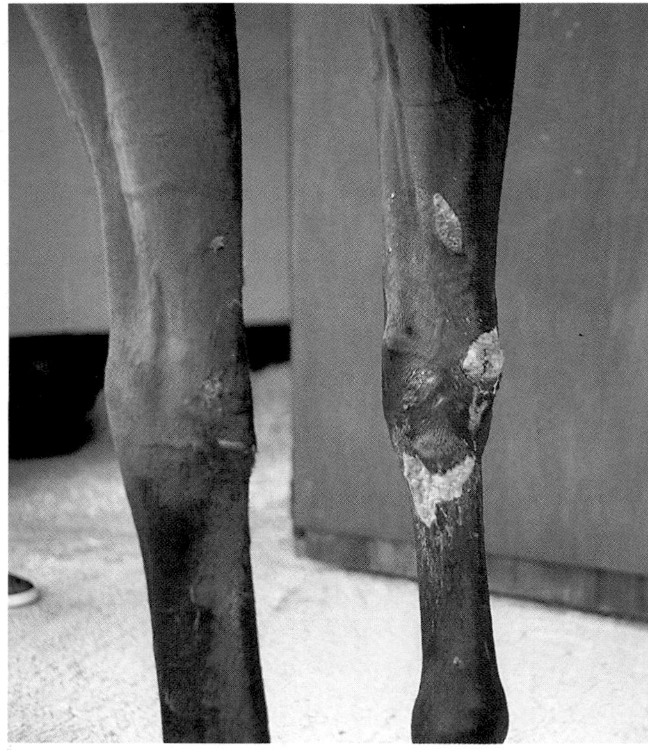

This extensive wound on the back of the knee has started to granulate, i.e. fill up with pink granulation tissue. This is second intention healing.

A permanently enlarged fetlock after a wound to the front has healed. This is merely a blemish and the horse was not lame.

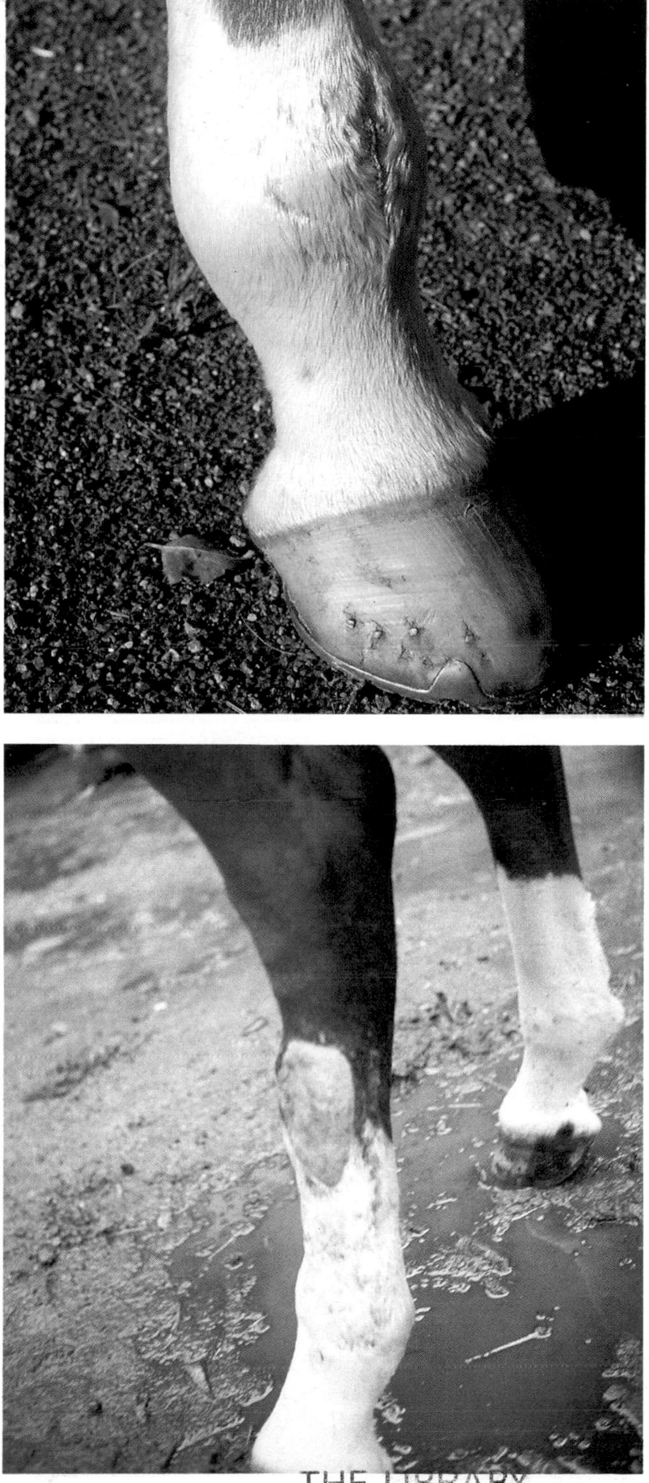

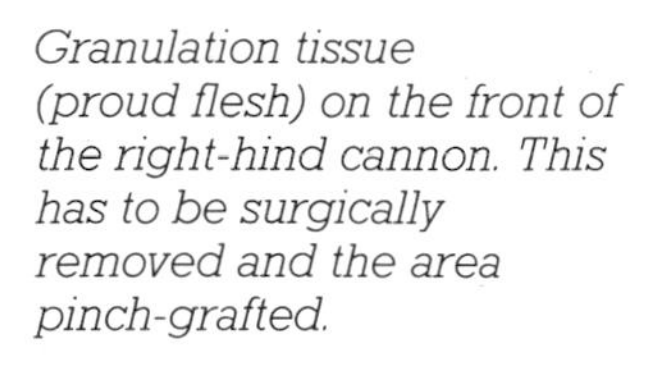

Granulation tissue (proud flesh) on the front of the right-hind cannon. This has to be surgically removed and the area pinch-grafted.

The acquired marks on the front left cannon and fetlock of this foal were caused by incorrectly applied bandages.

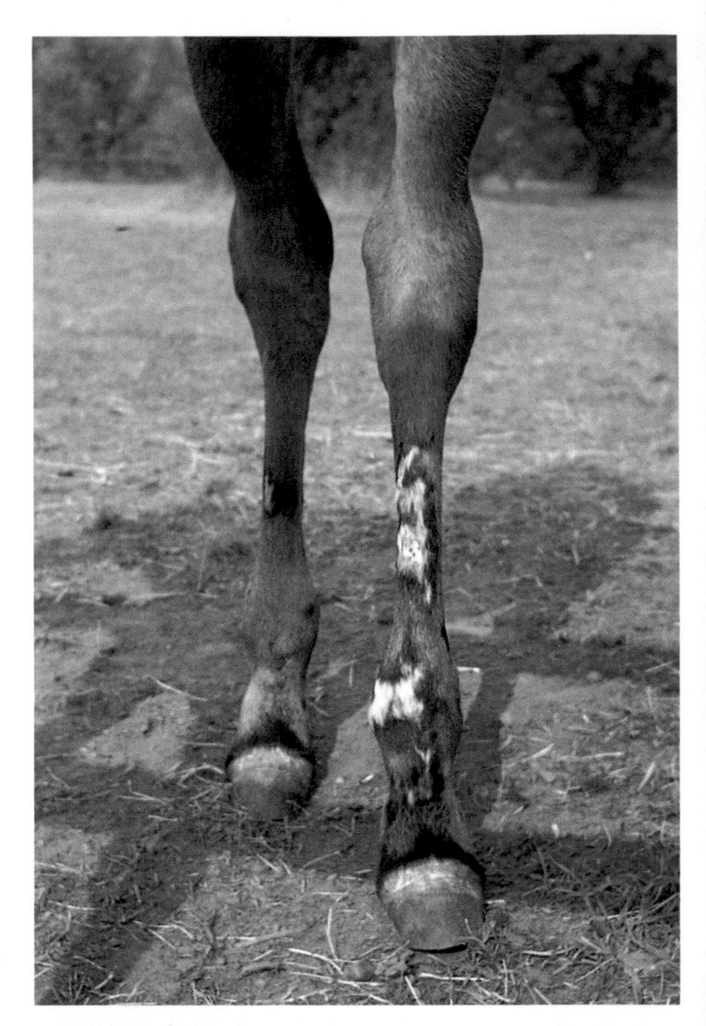

Left to right: knee, hock and fetlock stockings.

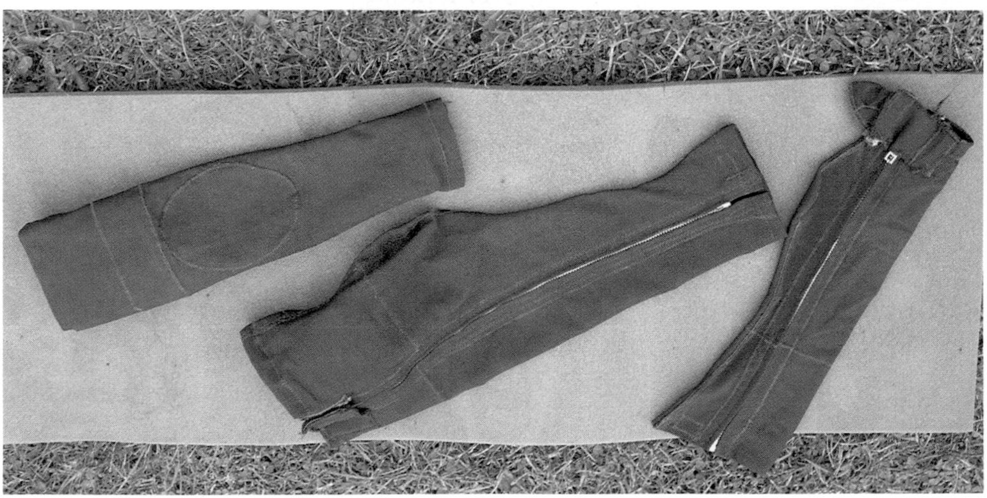

CHAPTER 7
DIGESTIVE DISORDERS AND FEEDING

A knowledge of the basic anatomy of the gut is important in understanding and preventing digestive disorders such as colic, choke and diarrhoea.

THE DIGESTIVE PROCESS

The alimentary tract is the tube in which digestion takes place. It includes the mouth, pharynx, oesophagus, stomach, small and large intestine and ends at the anus. Each area of the tract is responsible for a particular function in the digestive process, converting the food into substances that are easily absorbed into the blood stream and used by the cells of the body for energy, tissue-building and repair.

The lips and incisor (front) teeth take the food into the mouth, where it is broken into smaller pieces by the grinding action of the molar (cheek) teeth and mixed with saliva. Dental disease will effect this process.

The food moves to the back of the mouth (pharynx) and is swallowed, passing down the gullet (oesophagus) into the stomach. It is easy to locate the oesophagus on the left side of the horse's neck just behind the windpipe (trachea). It has muscular walls and the food material is propelled along by waves of contraction (peristalsis).

If material becomes lodged in the oesophagus causing a blockage, the saliva produced in the mouth eventually overflows from the oesophagus and pours

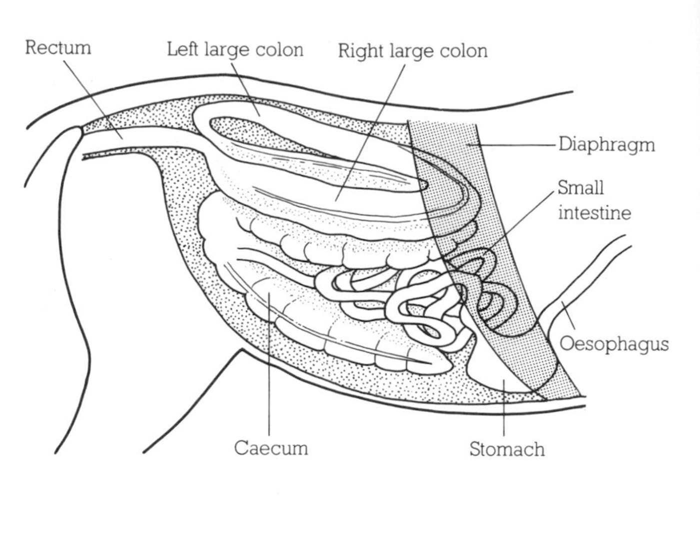

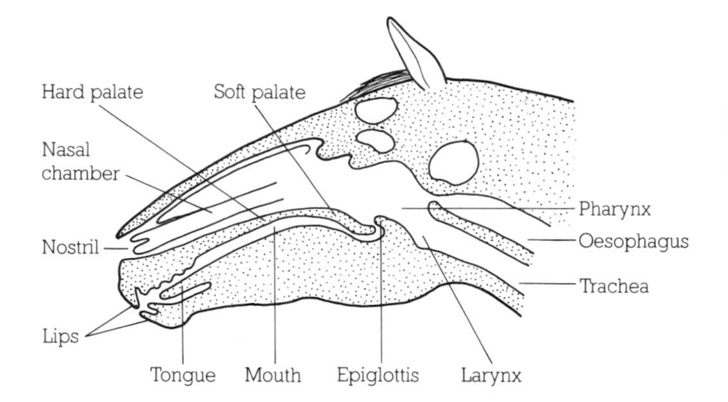

Fig. 50. The digestive tract – a cross-section of the head and neck showing the first part of the alimentary tract

out of the nostrils. This liquid may contain particles of the food which is causing the blockage. This condition is called **choke** and requires veterinary attention. Eating unsoaked (dry) sugar beet cubes is a common cause of choke.

The stomach lies within the rib cage and is relatively small, holding 8–15 litres (14–26 pt) of liquid. The starch (carbohydrate) in the food material is broken down by enzymes in the acidic gastric juices. Carbohydrates provide the energy for all cellular activities, and excess carbohydrates are stored as fat or as glycogen, which is an easily accessible energy source. Glycogen is found in muscle cells and in the liver. Another enzyme in the gastric juice, pepsin, starts to break down the protein in the food.

These partly digested contents pass into the small intestines which are up to 22 m (72 ft) long and have a capacity of 40–50 litres (70–88 pt). The enzymes from the pancreas and bile from the liver are released into the small intestines to continue the digestion of protein, fat and carbohydrate. The contents are in a liquid state and pass quickly into the first part of the large intestine, the caecum, via the ileo-caecal valve.

CHECKLIST – SIGNS OF ALIMENTARY TRACT DISORDERS

Loss of appetite
Weight loss
Debility and depression
Raised temperature, pulse and respiratory rate
Abdominal pain (colic) mild → severe
Diarrhoea or constipated
Blood or mucus in faeces
Alteration in gut sounds and motility
Abnormal stance
Abnormal behaviour

POSSIBLE CAUSES

Internal parasites	e.g.	Strongyles
Dental problem	e.g.	Sharp points on cheek teeth
Intestinal obstruction	e.g.	Impaction
Bacterial infection	e.g.	Salmonella

PREVENTION

Regular treatment with anthelmintics
Routine dental care
Feed good-quality ration at regular intervals
Isolate all horses with diarrhoea
Avoid stress

NURSING

Follow veterinary instructions regarding diet

FOR HORSES WITH BOWEL INFECTIONS

Provide disinfectant footbaths and rope off stables if salmonella is suspected
Wear protective clothing
Monitor horse's condition – regular TPR
Bandage tail to prevent it becoming contaminated with faecal material

The caecum is a large pear-shaped organ with a capacity of 30 litres (53 pt) situated on the right side of the abdomen. It joins the large colon at the caecal-colic opening. By listening over the right flank of the horse it is possible to hear caecal sounds. This is where bacteria break down the cellulose and fibre in the food to produce simple substances called free fatty acids. These are absorbed into the blood stream and converted into useable proteins, carbohydrates and fats.

Plant material contains varying amounts of cellulose. The type and amount of food fed to the horse directly affects the type and number of bacteria in the caecum and colon. Sudden changes in diet upset this delicate balance of necessary bacteria and leads to digestive disturbances.

The colon consists of two loops with a capacity of 60 litres (106 pt) and a length of 3 metres (10 ft). The right colon runs downwards and forward from the caecal colic opening to the diaphragm and then moves across to the left side of the abdomen to travel back to the pelvis. Here it takes a 180° turn on itself and reduces in diameter. This area is called the pelvic flexure and is a common site for food to impact. The upper loop of the left colon goes forward to the diaphragm again and travels back on the right side towards the pelvis, where it becomes narrower as it joins the small colon, which is 3.5 metres (11½ ft) in length.

Faecal balls are formed in the small colon as this is the site for water to be removed into the circulation. If the gut movements (peristalsis) are slow, more water is absorbed so the contents become too dry, but if the gut is over-active the contents will be watery, resulting in diarrhoea.

Impaction

There are three likely sites for food to become impacted in the large bowel. The first is the rounded head of the caecum. If the caecum is impacted there will be a reduction in the gut sounds when listening over the right flank. The other two sites are: the point where there is a sudden reduction in diameter of the alimentary tube, that is, at the pelvic flexure of the left colon; and at the junction of the large and small colon.

These impactions consist of accumulations of coarse, dry, undigested food that cause a partial or complete blockage in the gut. They are often caused by poor feeding and management. Poor-quality forage is fibrous and undigestible and more likely to become impacted. Foreign material which is undigestible may be eaten by young, curious animals and starving animals. Inadequate exercise and sudden changes from grass to a dry forage may lead to impactions. Dental disease and sharp teeth may prevent the horse grinding up coarse forage, so it reaches the large intestine in a form which the micro-organisms cannot digest.

Horses with a **large-intestine impaction** will show signs of abdominal pain, i.e., **colic**. The animal will be dull, restless, roll about, look at its flanks, dig up the bed, pass faeces infrequently and have reduced gut sounds. The pulse rate will be higher than normal and the horse will probably be sweating and reluctant to eat. Any horse showing signs of colic, however mild, must receive veterinary attention.

Owners must not administer any type of colic drink or drench. These products are dangerous and have no place in modern veterinary medicine.

THE HORSE'S NATURAL FEEDING PATTERN

Free-range horses spend up to 12 hours a day grazing, depending on the availability and quality of the pasture. The size of the grazing range is related to the proximity of water (in the wild, horses may travel 32 km/20 miles a day to find water). In restricted grazing areas such as small paddocks, there will be close-cropped 'lawns', and 'roughs' of long grass where the horses defaecate (pass dung). These roughs consist of unpalatable grass species, and because of faecal contamination are not normally grazed unless the animals are starving.

When deciding what, when and how to feed a horse, it is best to mimic as far as possible the way it would naturally eat. Normally horses eat small amounts of roughage at frequent intervals because of the small size of their stomachs. Digestion is more efficient if the stomach is not overfull.

The horse evolved as a grazing animal and the alimentary tract is designed to digest roughage, e.g., grass and hay. Fibre is essential for the gut to function correctly. It stimulates gut movement and breaks up the doughy mass that concentrates on their own would form.

Forage Feeds

Fig. 51. Different types of grass found in pasture land

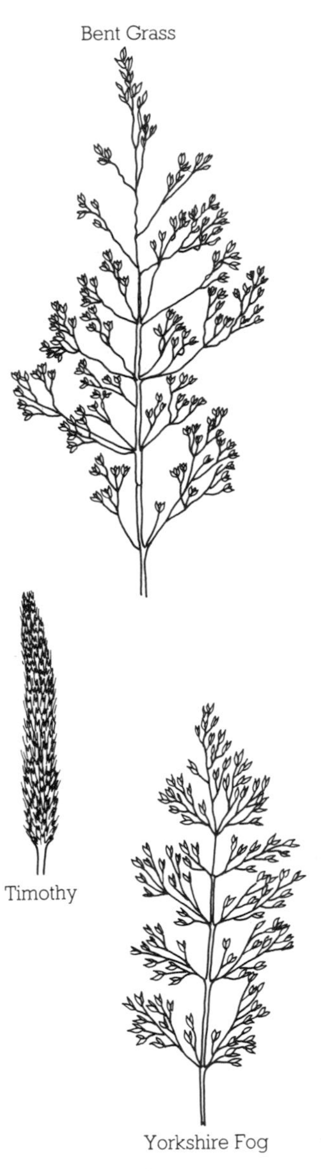

The amount of fibre, protein, calcium and the digestibility of the grass and hay varies from field to field. As the fibre content of the plant increases, its digestibility decreases, so less of the nutrients are available for the animal.

There are many types of hay: legume hay, e.g., lucerne; grass hay, seed hay, e.g., rye grass; and meadow hay made from permanent pasture.

Good-quality hay should be clean, highly palatable, smell sweet, feel smooth, pliable and dry, and be well harvested from good grass. Early-cut hay has a higher leaf content and therefore more protein. Good legume hay properly made will be higher in protein and calcium and provide more energy than grass hay. Poor-quality legume hay tends to be mouldy and dusty, and has less leaf than grass hay. Good grass hay contains species such as timothy, rye grass and meadow fescue. Meadow hay tends to include more varieties of grass, e.g., cocksfoot, white clover and herbs such as yarrow, chicory, dandelion and plantain. It may also contain weeds such as dock and thistle and poisonous plants. Some poisonous plants, such as ragwort, will be avoided by horses while growing on the pasture, but become quite palatable when mixed in the hay.

Poor-quality hay will contain less leaf and more fibrous stems. It has less protein and may be unpalatable. Bad hay is musty, mouldy, smells stale and contains many weeds and poisonous plants. It may show signs of weathering, either excess wetting or overbaking, and be black or have mildew on it. Some of these moulds and fungal spores cause respiratory problems, digestive disturbances and toxic poisoning. In addition bales may contain inedible rubbish especially those from fields near public roads where junk may have been thrown. Poor-quality, bad hay should never be fed to any livestock.

As bales come in many sizes and sections vary greatly in width, and as hay-nets can hold varying amounts, the hay should be weighed using a spring balance prior to feeding. One of the benefits of feeding hay is that it takes the horse longer to eat it

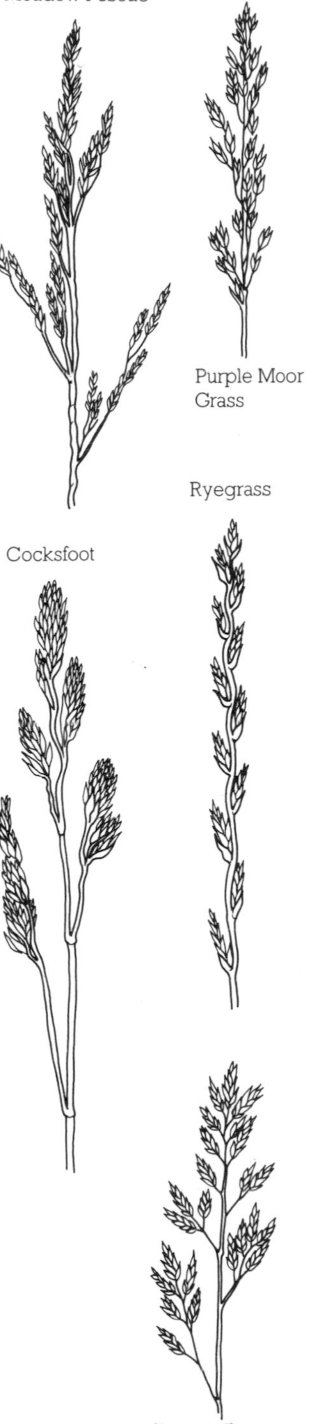

than concentrates, and so keeps the stabled horse occupied.

Adult animals in good condition and a little light work may be fed entirely on good-quality grass or hay with access to a salt lick and fresh water.

Good grazing pasture should include the following grasses: perennial rye grasses, timothy, smooth-stalked meadow grass, meadow fescues, cocksfoot, white and red clover. The nutritive value of the pasture depends on its palatability, amount of leaf and digestibility. Obviously the species of grass, soil type, climate and the time of year will effect the growth and flowering of the grass.

In the spring and autumn there is usually a flush of grass that has a lot of leaf and is high in digestible nutrients. Some species, such as timothy, remain leafy well into the summer and flower late. During a dry summer only the fibrous flowering stems are available for grazing and these are less palatable and have less protein. It may be necessary to supplement the diet of growing and breeding stock with extra protein at this time.

While the horse is grazing, it is also exercising itself and has the benefit of being in the fresh air rather than a dusty stable. If it is in the sunshine, it will also be producing vitamin D.

A number of other forage feeds have gained popularity over the last few years as an alternative to grass and hay. These include silage, hayage, chaff or chop with molasses, dried grass meal and lucerne nuts, treated straw and hydroponic grass.

BRAN AND SUGARBEET

Bran and sugarbeet are both by-products from the food industry.

Wheat bran adds bulk and fibre to the feed and has been added to horse rations since the mid-nineteenth century. It has a calcium/phosphorus imbalance, being high in phosphorus, which 'locks' up the calcium in the diet and prevents its absorption from the gut. Too much bran causes the bone disease **nutritional secondary hyperparathyroidism** (Bighead or Millers Disease).

Bran should only be fed if a calcium supplement or sugarbeet is added to the ration. The old-fashioned

17. Weighing a hay-net using a spring balance.

idea of giving a bran mash with epsom salts once a week goes against one of the most important rules of feeding – that changes in diet should not be sudden. If a mash is required for a sick animal, grass meal or bread meal with sugarbeet or molasses and chaff is much better than bran.

Sugarbeet is a by-product from the refining of sugar. It can be purchased as a dried pulp or dry nuts and has to be soaked for 12–24 hours prior to feeding. It is high in fibre and sugar and rich in calcium so it is useful to add to cereal rations. It is also rich in salt and has about the same amount of protein as good grass hay.

Feeding unsoaked sugarbeet is one of the commonest causes of choke (see page 66). Sugarbeet that has been soaked during hot weather, may start to ferment and must be thrown away.

Because both sugarbeet and bran will absorb water they are used to bulk up rations and prevent horses bolting their feed. They also act as mild laxatives.

CONCENTRATES

Most horses' diets include concentrates, which are low in fibre but high in nutrients, as well as forage. Most concentate feeds include the cereal grains, oats, barley and maize. They are all low in calcium. Oats contain the most fibre and maize has the most starch (energy). They provide the extra protein needed for the growing and breeding animal, and the extra carbohydrate or energy for the working horse. It is important to feed a sufficient amount of a balanced ration to keep the horse in a good bodily condition and capable of performing athletically to the standard required of it. For example adult horses only require about 8 per cent protein in their diet where as young immature horses need around 16 per cent.

If the horse is underfed for its work load, it will use its own body fat to supply the energy (calories) it needs to perform. When all the fat has been used, it will then start breaking down muscle tissue to provide energy. If the horse is overfed, as many horses are, the excess carbohydrate (calories) will be stored as body fat.

Commercial horse feeds are either pelleted into cubes or nuts, or fed as coarse mixes. They are specially formulated by the manufacturers to provide a balanced diet when fed with forage for each specific group of animals, e.g., Horse and Pony cubes, Stud cubes, Event cubes, etc.

Some cubes contain forage as well as cereals, so are known as a 'complete feed'. They are used for animals with respiratory allergies, but as they are quickly eaten they lead to boredom vices in the stabled horse. The complete feed cubes are not always palatable and some horses refuse to eat them.

Bags of feed should be stored in a cool dry place away from vermin and livestock (many horses have had serious colic after breaking into the feed-store and helping themselves). Check the sell-by date before opening each new bag of feed. The contents should appear normal for that brand, have no unusual smell and not be dusty or mouldy or stale.

If a horse is reluctant to eat a feed that it usually enjoys, and does not appear to be ill, it may be that the feed has something wrong with it. Occasionally the wrong feed does get into the wrong bag at the mill, e.g., cattle-formulated feed in a horse feed bag. Feeds especially formulated for other species of animals should *never* be fed to horses.

FEEDING GUIDELINES

The commercial feeds, if fed according to the manufacturers' directions, will provide the horse with the correct amount of vitamins and minerals. However, if bran and other feedstuffs are added to these balanced feeds, they may unbalance the horse's diet. The suggested amounts to be fed, given on the feed packs, are a rough guide only; much depends on the existing body condition and amount of work the animal does – the more exercise the horse has, the more calories it will need; and conversely, the less exercise, the less calories.

All concentrate feed should be fed by weight, not by volume, as a scoop may hold 1 kg (2 lb) of a dense food and only 0.5 kg (1 lb) of a high-volume food. Scoops also come in various sizes, which can be misleading! It often sounds as if an animal is getting plenty to eat until the food is actually weighed, and it turns out to be very little. The obvious way to tell if a horse is getting the correct amount to eat is by looking at its condition and adjusting its feed according to the condition-score (see page 32).

It is vital to feed at regular intervals and avoid sudden changes in the diet. Horses which are left for many hours without food are more likely to bolt their food, causing digestive disorders. They are also more likely to develop depraved appetites, e.g., eating dung, and also vices such as crib-biting and chewing wood.

Avoid exercising a horse immediately after feeding, as exercise interferes with the digestive process and causes discomfort. Tired animals should not be given large feeds or large amounts of cold water immediately after strenuous exercise. They should be allowed to cool down and relax with a small amount of hay and a small volume of lukewarm water.

It is dangerous to give too much carbohydrate to a horse that is not in work. The horse may suffer from azoturia (see page 86) when it starts work again. If for any reason a horse which is normally in work has to be laid off, even for one day, its ration must be adjusted. Overfeeding in general may cause obesity, colic and laminitis!

CHECKLIST – FEEDING

DOS

DO feed measured amounts by weight

DO feed good-quality forage and concentrates

DO feed at regular intervals – at least twice a day

DO store feed correctly in a locked room

DO avoid sudden changes in diet

DO use clean bowls and buckets

DO feed according to condition and exercise

DO condition-score regularly

DO allow access to clean water at all times

DO feed balanced rations

DO reduce the ration when exercise is reduced

DON'TS

DO NOT use spoiled, mouldy, out-of-date food

DO NOT feed immediately before or after exercise

DO NOT allow bullying at feed times

DO NOT feed excess protein to working horses

DO NOT feed excess calories (carbohydrate) to obese or idle horses

DO NOT overdose with vitamin A and vitamin D

FEEDING THE THIN HORSE

When a number of thin horses are seen on one premises it is usually a sign of poor management. The pasture may be over-grazed, or the quality or quantity of hay being fed is inadequate. The animals may not be on a worming programme, or they may be lousy.

Sometimes just one horse is thin in an otherwise healthy-looking group. This animal may be bullied by the others and does not get its share of the feed. It may be young and growing, and need more protein to put on flesh; or it may be elderly and need special feeding to maintain its body condition.

Under-feeding is a problem associated with the inexperienced owner. This is common when they sell a small, native-type pony, which is hard to under-feed, and buy a larger horse that is not such a good doer and needs a lot more feed.

Other causes of thinness include dental problems, such as diseased or missing teeth, parrot mouths and sharp cheek teeth, which may all slow down the rate of eating and prevent proper chewing of the food. Horses that are not provided with shelter in bad weather will not graze, and they burn up calories trying to maintain their body temperature, so may become thin. Horses which are overworked for their plane of nutrition will lose weight.

If the horse is showing other signs of ill health as well as being underweight, you should seek veterinary assistance immediately. The horse's diet must be checked to see if it is receiving an adequate amount of food. The quality of the ration should also be inspected, as poor-quality food has a poor nutritional value.

A thin horse must be fed on its own and the number of daily feeds increased to three or four. Any change in diet must be gradual, and include good-quality forage and a balanced concentrate mix including a vitamin supplement. Its teeth should be rasped and any parasitic conditions treated. The horse should be provided with shelter and rugged up. It should only be given very light walking exercise, preferably in hand as it is difficult to fit a saddle on a thin animal without causing pressure rubs.

If the horse's body condition does not improve over three to four weeks, a further veterinary examination will be necessary.

FEEDING THE FAT HORSE

Overweight horses are a common problem. Fat animals cannot perform as athletes. They put unnecessary strains and stresses on their limbs, lungs and heart. If young, immature animals carry too much weight, this may cause permanent damage to their joints and limbs, resulting in lameness. Fat brood mares are not as fertile and have more problems at parturition (foaling). Overweight animals are a greater anaesthetic and surgical risk than those of correct body-weight. Horses with respiratory problems and limb injuries take longer to recover if they are obese.

Many small native ponies are overweight because they are given access to unlimited rich grazing and are given inadequate exercise. These ponies are prime candidates for laminitis (see page 44).

Fat animals must be put on restricted grazing, and given a reduced ration. The quality of the hay can be changed to a lower-calorie hay, e.g., meadow hay instead of legume hay. A bare paddock or a menage or a yard is a useful place to let the horse wander about in. If this is not available, the animal will have to be stabled on shavings and fed small amounts of hay and about half its maintenance level of feed. Periods of exercise should be interspersed between the small feeds to prevent boredom if the animal is stabled. The exercise can be gradually increased to two or three 30-minute sessions a day at a brisk walk, and after three weeks include a few short bursts of trot.

It may be impossible to keep a saddle in place on a very fat animal so the exercise will have to be on a lunge, long reins or in-hand until it has lost some weight.

Very sudden strict diets can in themselves cause serious problems, such as hyperlipaemia, which is often fatal. In this condition, fat globules are seen in the blood stream as the animal mobilizes its own fat to provide energy.

POINTS ON WINTER FEEDING

Pasture is nutritionally poor in winter. At this time, it is necessary to condition score (see page 32) every couple of weeks by palpation, as a thick coat can cover a thin body. The coat should be examined for lice as heavy infestations cause anaemia and weight loss.

In cold and windy conditions the horse's nutritional maintenance requirements increase. If shelters and rugs are provided, the quantity of extra food required will be less than for animals exposed to bad weather. Sometimes owners who are well wrapped up in layers of clothing forget just how cold it is. Some stables are poorly positioned and extremely draughty, and the horse is virtually standing in a wind tunnel. The chill factor is high in these conditions, and the horse will burn up calories in keeping warm. High-energy food must be given if the horse is to maintain its body condition. In addition, animals that are stressed by climatic conditions are more prone to respiratory infections.

In winter it is common for horses to suffer from colic after drinking icy water. Sometimes, they are deprived of water altogether for many hours, because it freezes over, and then over-indulge when they have free access to it. If the ground is covered in snow, provide extra forage as well as a concentrate ration.

VITAMINS

Vitamins are organic compounds that are required in small amounts for the body to function normally. They are divided into 2 groups: the fat-soluble vitamins, A, D, E and K, which can be stored in the liver and body fat; and the water-soluble B complex and C. Vitamins which are not normally stored in body tissue have to be supplied regularly.

Healthy adult horses on a good-quality ration are unlikely to have a vitamin deficiency. Vitamin B complex, E and K are found in sufficient amounts in forage and cereals. The micro-organisms in the caecum and colon synthesize (make) B vitamins and vitamin K. Vitamin C is produced in the horse's liver, and the precursor to vitamin D is found in the skin which, on exposure to ultraviolet light, forms vitamin D.

Good sources of vitamin A are carrots, lucerne hay and green pasture. The horse's supply of vitamin A and D are subject to seasonal fluctuations, and may need supplementing in the winter months.

Deficiencies in vitamins are usually a result of feeding poor-quality rations. Prolonged storage of feed, excess heat and light all destroy vitamins. Sick and stressed animals have an increased requirement for vitamins, as do young animals, lactating mares and those in late pregnancy. Horses in winter time and those stabled for long periods may need extra vitamins. The prolonged use of antibiotics may disturb the gut flora and suppress the micro-organisms which normally produce the B complex group.

If the horse is fed too large a quantity of the water-soluble vitamins, the excess will be excreted. However, the fat-soluble vitamins A and D are toxic if present in large amounts. So apart from wasting money by feeding an excess of vitamins, actual harm can be done. Excess vitamin A causes bone deformities, and excess vitamin D causes mineralization of the heart and blood vessels.

Vitamins are used in the treatment of certain diseases. Bracken poisoning is treated with Thiamine a B vitamin and warfarin poisoning is treated with vitamin K. Vitamin E and selenium have been used in the treatment and prevention of azoturia.

MINERALS

Four per cent of the horse's body-weight is mineral matter, approximately 70 per cent of which is calcium and phosphorus. The essential minerals are calcium,

VITAMIN GUIDE

Vitamin	Feed with good level	Feed with poor level
A	Carrots All green feed Good-quality hay, especially legume hay	Cereals Old hay Poorly made hay
B group	Grass, lucerne, grain, brewers' yeast Synthesized in large intestine	Poorly made hay
C	Synthesized in horse's tissue	——
D	Sun cured hay Skin and ultraviolet light Fish oil	Cereal
E	Cereals Green forage Hay	——

phosphorus, potassium, sodium, chlorine and magnesium. The trace elements, required in smaller amounts, consist of cobalt, iron, zinc, copper, manganese, iodine, molybdenum and selenium. These minerals are essential in the diet as the horse cannot manufacture them itself, unlike some of the vitamins. They play a vital role in the horse's metabolism.

Balanced proprietary feeds contain the minerals required by the horse in the correct proportions. If mineral supplements are added to these feeds, the accurate balance of minerals will be destroyed.

Salt is the main basic supplement. It is often used with the trace element iodine, and may be given as a trace-mineralized salt lick. A horse that has a tendency towards wood-chewing will often stop if salt is included in its ration. Sodium, chlorine and potassium are necessary in maintaining the pH and fluid balance within the body.

Sulphur is found in the amino acids (building blocks for protein) methionine and cystine. Methionine is essential for good quality horn and hair production. Magnesium is present in bran and most vegetable protein. It is involved in calcium and phosphorus metabolism. Magnesium and calcium salts are used in horses to treat travel stress.

The common dietary mineral imbalance that occurs in horses is that of calcium and phosphorus. These should be fed in a ratio of 1.7 calcium to 1.0 phosphorus. Both elements are essential in the structure of normal bones and teeth.

CHAPTER 8
EXERCISE

Exercise is important for humans and horses alike, whatever their age. Regular, moderate exercise keeps them in good physical condition.

Free-range horses spend 18 hours out of a 24-hour period awake and alert, of which 12 hours is spent grazing and therefore taking exercise. Unfortunately many horses spend 23 out of every 24 hours in a stable, only being exercised for an hour a day if they are lucky. No human athlete would consider competing at any level if they could only exercise for 1 hour a day and had to remain in an area the size of a telephone box for the other 23 hours! Horses which are kept out at grass and ridden occasionally are physically and mentally better off than the permanently stabled and confined horse.

Occasional ridden exercise should be slow and gentle if injuries such as muscle strains, tendon and ligament damage are to be avoided. Remember that a person can always stop exercising if they feel tired or start to ache, but the horse may not be given this choice. When thinking about preparing a horse for an athletic career, the same considerations should apply as for a human athlete.

The aim of training, conditioning or fitness programmes is to prepare the musculo-skeletal systems (bones, muscles, tendons, etc.), the cardiovascular system (heart and blood vessels), and the respiratory system (lungs), for the work which is demanded of them in a particular sport.

PREVENTION OF INJURIES

Prevention and early detection of athletic injuries is of paramount importance during training. A horse with good conformation, when correctly trained, is more likely to stay sound and have the ability to perform athletically. Conformational defects nearly always cause problems if the horse is asked to perform at a high standard of athletic prowess. Animals which are unprepared for exercise or have an inadequate warm-up period, or become fatigued are more likely to sustain injuries.

Most injuries occur because of lack of fitness, poor conformation, badly fitting tack, bad conditions underfoot, an inexperienced or incapable rider, and accidents. Whatever pursuit the horse is eventually going to be used for, it must have good basic training. It should be adequately schooled so that it is supple, balanced, co-ordinated and obedient in all paces. The early training of the horse will also affect its mental attitude to work.

An inexperienced rider can easily unbalance and hinder the horse physically and confuse it mentally. Riders' errors over jumps, and especially at speed,

Fig. 52. Some of the main muscles of the horse

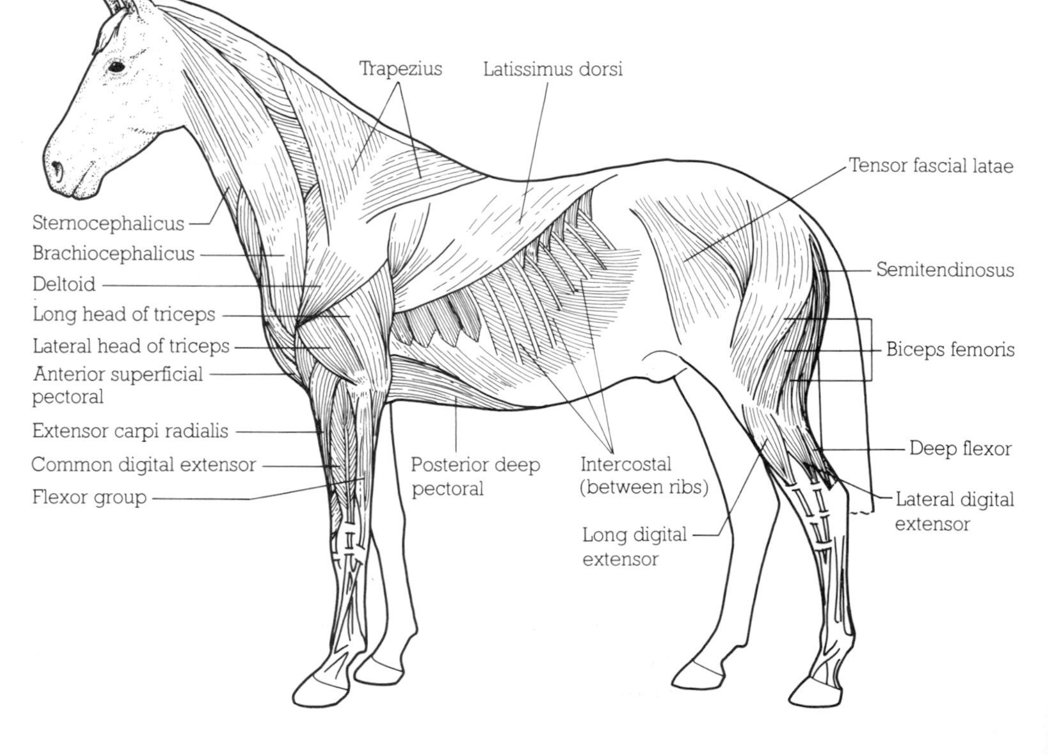

CHECKLIST – SIGNS OF MUSCULO-SKELETAL PROBLEMS

Lameness
Heat and swelling
Pain on flexing or extending joints
Pain when weight-bearing
Pain on palpation
Abnormal gait
Foot not landing correctly
Abnormal wear on shoe
Reluctant to move
Loss of athletic performance
Abnormal stance at rest, e.g., resting or pointing a foot

CAUSES

Exercise induced	e.g.	Sprains, strains
Accidental trauma	e.g.	Wounds, fractures
Obesity/dietary	e.g.	Laminitis, azoturia
Infection	e.g.	Pedal sepsis, mud rash

FIRST AID/NURSING

Box rest/controlled exercise
Support bandages
Prevent further injury

can cause bad accidents. In addition, chronic stress is seen in those that are ridden in an inconsistent manner, as they do not know how to avoid being punished for their 'bad behaviour', which is in fact the result of bad riding.

Badly fitting tack causes discomfort, pain and injuries that will affect the horse's way of going and make exercise unpleasant. Exercise boots must be fitted with care. Some designs have very tight elasticated straps which cause damage to the underlying skin. In severe cases the skin actually dies, leaving an open wound.

Horses are expected to exercise on all sorts of surfaces, some of which are far from ideal. Roads and baked ground are too hard to work on except at the walk. Trotting on hard surfaces jars the limbs and increases the wear and tear on the lower limb joints. Uneven and irregular surfaces are difficult to travel over and may cause strains and sprains to muscles and joints. Muscle, tendon and ligament injuries are common when the conditions underfoot are heavy and deep, such as ploughed fields or deep sand.

Artificial surfaces, if well maintained and not too deep, should be ideal to work and compete on. Many different materials are used on menages and exercise tracks; some are 'springy' and others are 'dead' to ride on. Whatever the surface, it should be level, have a regular consistency and depth.

The commonest reason for loss of athletic performance and exercise intolerance are diseases of the respiratory and musculo-skeletal system. Respiratory problems can be kept to a minimum by keeping to vaccination programmes, avoiding contact with infected animals and premises, feeding good clean forage, removing dust and irritating fumes from the horse's environment and avoiding stress and chilling. Horses which are clipped or normally rugged may easily become chilled in transit and hanging around on show grounds.

Airway resistance is increased with respiratory disease. The horse uses more energy to overcome this when exercising. Horses with broken wind (COPD) have higher heart rates on exercise than normal horses. Therefore the heart muscle has to work harder.

Young immature animals should not be worked or over-lunged, as this can cause permanent damage to their limbs, as can carrying excess body-weight. Old animals on the other hand need frequent, slow exercise to prevent muscle wastage and stiffness. Massage and grooming will also help tone up muscle.

AEROBIC AND ANAEROBIC EXERCISE

Muscle contraction during exercise involves large amounts of chemical energy being converted into mechanical energy. This energy is formed by two processes, an aerobic pathway (using oxygen) and an anaerobic pathway (works without oxygen). Oxygen is needed to release energy from circulating glucose and fatty acids, glycogen from the muscle cells and stored triglycerides (fatty acids) from the fat tissue. The anaerobic process uses circulating glucose and muscle glycogen to provide energy.

Depending on the type, duration and intensity of the exercise, varying amounts of energy is released from a balance of these two processes. Intense exercise such as high-speed sprints mainly uses anaerobic pathways to produce the energy for muscle activity, whereas endurance exercise involves more of the aerobic production of energy.

Anaerobic pathways produce *lactate* in the muscle cells, which lowers the pH of the cell so making it more acidic, and stops further energy production. When the glycogen stores are used up, muscle fatigue occurs. The greater the horse's ability to produce energy aerobically, the less lactate accumulates, so muscle fatigue takes longer to develop.

Training increases the muscle cells' ability to store and use energy, and the number of small blood vessels (capillaries) between the muscle fibres, and the amount of oxygen carried in the blood. The musculo-skeletal system takes longer to show an increase in strength, mass and fitness; i.e., it does not respond as quickly as the energy system to training.

TRAINING PROGRAMMES

A training programme should be specially designed for each horse, as they are all individuals. It will depend on the type of sport the horse will be involved in, and should improve its performance in that sport. The programme should include basic schooling prior to training for the horse's specialist activity. The ultimate test for any training programme is the animal's ability to perform well in the event for which it has been trained.

There are two main types of training, *continuous* and *intermittent* or *interval* training.

In continuous training, each session consists of a single exercise period; the intensity and length of the work alters from day to day as the animal becomes fitter. It has been shown with human athletes that those who train four or five times a week show greater improvement than those who only train two or three times weekly. Continuous training is often used for endurance work and for conventional sprint training.

The duration and frequency of the exercise appears to be as important as the intensity when fittening endurance horses.

Intermittent or interval training involves a series of exercise bouts interspersed with short periods of rest or walking. Horses must undergo a conditioning programme prior to interval training because the work is quite hard and they could easily become injured. Interval training enables the horse to undergo more high-intensity work than it could normally stand with continuous programmes. The rest periods allow the horse's muscles to recover so that more work can be done without fatigue. The heart rate is monitored in the rest period.

Horses which have been successfully interval-trained are less susceptible to musculo-skeletal injuries. They tend to reach the acquired level of fitness faster than using traditional methods, and can maintain a given speed for a longer period.

Repetition training involves repeated bouts of slow-speed exercise followed by rest periods of variable length. These help the animal to pace itself, improve its strength and muscular co-ordination. This method is used to train event horses. The horse may be asked to trot 3.2 km (2 miles) then walk 1.6 km (1 mile), and this is repeated three or four times. Jogging and submaximal exercise helps strengthen the limb bones.

Performance-testing is widely used on human athletes and is available for élite horses. Performance-testing monitors heart rate and oxygen uptake during graded exercise on a treadmill. The enzyme activity in the skeletal muscles is measured to detect lactate levels. The horse's gait can be analysed for lameness using a force-plate or video camera. All these tests are helpful in assessing fitness and response to training, and for the early detection and prevention of injuries, as well as to improve performance. The constant attention to detail in the care and training of the horse should mean less injuries and a fitter animal.

External factors such as terrain, ambient temperature and humidity will affect the animal's response to exercise. Apart from lameness, horses may become exhausted, dehydrated (lack of fluid) and have electrolyte imbalances due to loss of mineral salts in the sweat.

Azoturia or **exertional rhabdomyolysis**, a cramp-like condition of the muscles of the loin and hindquarters, can occur during an exercise session. Carbohydrate overloading increases the glycogen level stored in the muscles, so when the animal is exercised again, there is a build up of lactate in the muscle cells. In mild cases, the horse may just appear to be slightly stiff or show a change in gait, but in severe cases it is extremely reluctant or unable to move. The muscles involved will feel hard and swollen, and will cause a lot of pain. The horse will have a high pulse and respiratory rate and sweat profusely. Its urine may be red to black in colour due to the presence of the pigment from the damaged muscle cells. This condition can easily be mistaken for a case of colic or laminitis.

Azoturia is frequently seen in animals which have had full rations although they have not been exercised as normal. It may also occur after a sudden increase in strenuous work, after travelling long distances, and at the end of endurance rides.

Although the mildest cases respond to gentle exercise, most horses with this condition should not be exerted or forced to walk, as this will cause further damage. The muscle pigment released from the damaged cells can damage the kidneys and cause kidney failure.

The horse must be travelled home in a box or trailer. While waiting for the vet, the horse should be kept warm and dry and stabled on a thick shavings bed. Hay and water should be placed close to the horse as it will be reluctant or unable to move.

The vet can monitor the muscle damage by taking a series of blood samples and measuring the amounts of muscle enzymes present. The horse should be rested until the enzyme levels have returned to a normal level. The management, especially feeding and exercise regimes, may have to be altered to prevent further attacks of azoturia.

COMMON INJURIES WHICH OCCUR DURING EXERCISE

Interference injuries, such as **brushing**, **overreaching** and **cross-firing**, are common in young unbalanced animals and those with conformational defects of the limbs. Various types of boots can be used on horses' legs to prevent them.

Fig. 53. Tendons and ligaments of the foreleg

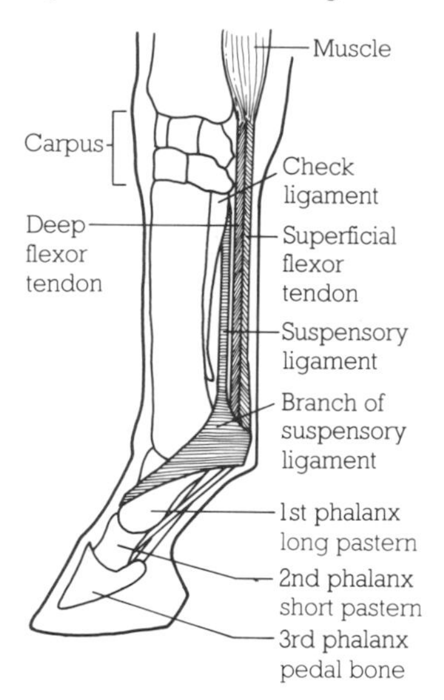

Strenuous exercise may result in strains to muscles, tendons and ligaments. Muscle fibres may be torn or damaged during a fall or blow. Muscle has a good blood supply, and frequently large bruises develop at the site of muscle trauma.

Tendons which attach the upper limb muscles to the lower limb bones can be overstretched and strained. Tendons have a poor blood supply and may take 12–18 months to heal once injured. Ligaments attach bone to bone, supporting the joint; when they are damaged, the joint becomes unstable. Sprained ligaments are painful as they are well supplied with sensory nerves, and are slow to heal because they have a poor blood supply.

These soft-tissue injuries require immediate first aid attention. Firm support bandages should be applied where possible to control the inflammatory swelling and prevent further damage by supporting the injured structure. Obviously movement must be restricted and the horse stabled. The horse will require veterinary attention. Acutely lame animals that are reluctant to bear weight on the injured limb will need support bandages on the other three legs and frog supports on the feet to prevent weight-bearing laminitis.

All sorts of pointless, barbaric methods have been

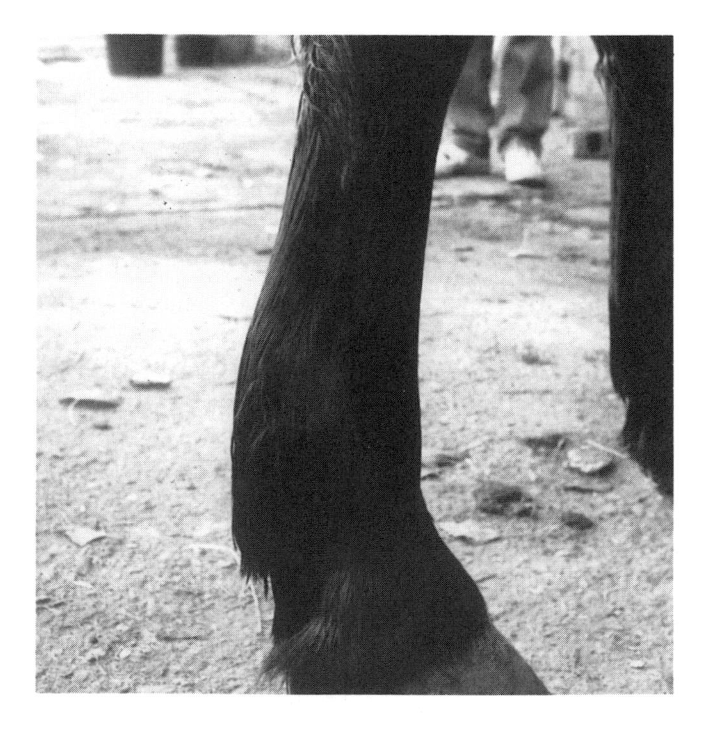

18. A bowed tendon. The flexor tendons which run down the back of the leg curve outwards just above the fetlock at the site of the injury.

tried in the past, without success, to hasten the repair process and ultimate recovery time of tendon injuries. These include firing, burning the skin over the tendon, pin firing (inserting red hot needles into the tendon) and blistering (damaging the overlaying skin with an irritant substance.). *None* of these procedures worked; they just caused further damage to the tendon and skin, and inflicted unnecessary pain on the horse. No human athlete would tolerate this type of 'treatment' and neither should the horse!

Bones may be fractured, that is, a crack passes across the bone from side to side. Some fractures require orthopaedic (bone) surgery using screws, plates and pins to hold the bone fragments closely together while they mend. Pieces of bone may be pulled off the edge of joints to form **chip fractures**, commonly seen in the carpal (knee) joints and fetlock joint. These chips may have to be surgically removed from the joint. Bones may be stressed and small cracks called **stress fractures** may result. These are common on the front of the cannon bone i.e. sore shins. Stress fractures require complete rest and support bandages, otherwise they will cause continual lameness.

Treatment

X-rays are commonly taken to assess bone and joint injuries. Ultrasound scanners and infra-red thermography (a way of measuring heat in tissues) are used to locate soft-tissue injuries. Electrical (Faradic) stimulation of muscle can be used to locate muscle damage.

All injuries cause inflammation, that is, an increased blood flow, to the area. Various cells in the blood limit the injury, remove the damaged tissue and repair the defect. The inflammatory response is recognized by heat, swelling, pain, redness (if the skin is involved) and loss of function. Most treatments aim to control this response and promote the repair process.

Massage, either manual or using sophisticated machines, may assist in dispersing the tissue-fluid (oedema) swelling associated with tissue injuries. Massage should not be used until all bleeding at the site has stopped.

Careful exercise involving physiotherapy techniques is most useful in the convalescence period. This aims to maintain fitness and strength in the muscles while the injury is healing.

SECTION 3
AVOIDING ILLNESS AND ACCIDENTS

CHAPTER 9
ROUTINE HEALTH PROCEDURES

VACCINATION

Tetanus

Routine vaccination is essential to protect horses against **tetanus** (lockjaw), which is caused by the bacteria *Clostridium tetani*. The horse is particularly susceptible to this extremely distressing disease.

The organism can live for many years in the soil as a spore. These spores are frequently taken in by the horse as it grazes and passed out again in the faeces. In anaerobic conditions, however, such as those found in the depths of wounds, the bacteria multiply and produce toxins that travel throughout the body via the nerves. These toxins destroy white blood cells and cause muscle spasm. The slightest sound or touch can stimulate a muscle spasm and generalized muscular stiffness, giving the horse a rocking-horse appearance. The horse is eventually unable to eat or swallow, and the respiratory muscles become affected. Most horses suffering from tetanus die of respiratory or heart failure, or exhaustion.

As 80 to 90 per cent of all clinical cases die, it is absolutely vital to protect all horses against this disease, by using the readily available *tetanus toxoid vaccine*.

The primary course consists of two doses given 4–6 weeks apart by deep intra-muscular injection, followed by a booster injection one year later. Subsequent boosters at 2-yearly intervals are necessary to provide the horse with an adequate level of antibodies. The tetanus toxoid is a dead vaccine and has few side effects.

If the vaccination status of a horse is unknown, a primary course should be started as soon as possible. If an unvaccinated horse is injured, an injection of *antitoxin* can be given to neutralize any toxins present. This will give a temporary protection for 2 to 3 weeks. It is normal practice to give the first dose of tetanus toxoid at the same time as the antitoxin, so that the horse starts to produce antibodies against the disease by the time the antitoxin's protection has waned. There may be side effects following the use of antitoxin, and it is far better to protect the horse by vaccination so that there is no need to use the antitoxin. Antitoxin is used along with antibiotics, muscle relaxants and sedatives to treat horses with the disease.

Equine Influenza

Most horses are also vaccinated against the viral disease **equine influenza**, of which there are several strains. It is a highly infectious disease of the respiratory system, and one strain produces a more severe clinical disease, including viral pneumonia. Secondary bacterial infection is common, and complications such as heart muscle disease and broken wind sometimes occur.

As with most diseases, stress, overcrowding, poor nutrition and poor management will affect the course and severity of the disease. The incubation period is about 5 days, so the disease can spread rapidly through a group of horses in a stable-yard. Affected horses shed virus in their nasal discharge and by coughing. They usually have a high fever and are therefore dull and have no appetite. They have a nasal discharge and a cough which may persist for weeks. All infected and in-contact horses should be isolated and completely rested for at least 1 month. After all respiratory signs have disappeared, animals with secondary complications such as heart disease and broken wind may require 6 months complete rest.

There are no specific drugs to treat equine influenza virus, so vaccination is an important and necessary means of control. It is important to vaccinate fit and healthy individuals in order to achieve a good level of protection. Animals which are debilitated at the time

CHECKLIST – SIGNS OF RESPIRATORY DISEASE

Raised temperature, pulse, respiratory rate
Laboured breathing
Nasal discharge
Sneezing, snorting and coughing
Occular discharge
Depressed, lethargic, loss of appetite
Roaring or rattling noises over windpipe
Enlarged glands
Exercise intolerance

POSSIBLE CAUSES

Virus	e.g.	Influenza
Bacteria	e.g.	Strangles
Parasite	e.g.	Lungworm
Allergy	e.g.	Fungal spores in hay

PREVENTION

Use available vaccines
Avoid stress and chilling
Provide well-ventilated stables
Keep dust and fungal spores to a minimum in bed and feed
Keep in good bodily condition
Avoid contact with infected animals
Treat all donkeys for lungworm infection

NURSING

Complete rest
Keep warm
Isolate if viral or bacterial infection
Damp all feed
Feed at ground level
Remove cause if possible
Keep in allergy-free environment
Keep nose and eyes clean
Use inhalations as prescribed

of vaccination are unlikely to produce a good immune response. Manufacturers design vaccines that give a strong immunity and are free from adverse side effects. They advise that vaccination should not take place immediately after exercise or travelling, and that following vaccination horses should not be stressed or physically exerted for a few days.

The basic vaccination programme consists of two injections 4 to 6 weeks apart with the first booster dose 6 months after the second injection. To obtain good protection, all horses should receive subsequent boosters at intervals of 6–9 months. Horses at high risk of infection, e.g., competition animals, should be boosted at 6-monthly intervals.

Reputable insurance companies require that all insured horses are fully vaccinated and routinely treated with anthelmintics as a disease prevention measure.

Equine influenza virus vaccines do not protect horses from other virus infections of the respiratory tract. Therefore vaccinated horses may develop respiratory diseases due to other causal agents.

DENTITION

When a foal reaches 9 months of age, it will have a full set of *milk* or *temporary* teeth. These consist of 6 *incisor* (front) teeth and 6 *premolar* teeth in the upper (*maxilla*) and lower (*mandible*) jaws. The space between the incisors and cheek teeth is the *interdental space* or *bars* of the mouth. The temporary incisors are rounded at the gum margin, very small and pearly white. The middle two incisors are the *centrals*, the tooth on either side is the *lateral* tooth and the ones on the outside of the laterals are the *corners*.

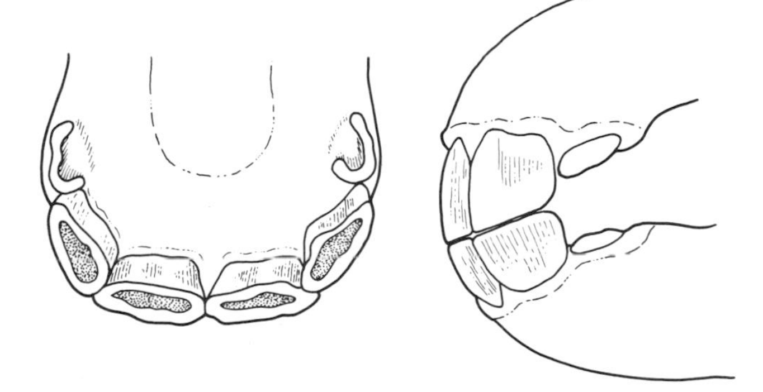

Fig. 54. Dentition of a 9-month-old foal

The *permanent* or *adult* incisor teeth erupt at specific ages in most horses. The central incisors erupt at 2½ years of age, the laterals at 3½ years and the corners at 4½ years. The teeth in the upper jaw usually erupt before those in the lower jaw and are larger. They are in wear with the incisors on the opposite jaw approximately 6 months after erupting: at 3 years, 4 years and 5 years respectively. The permanent incisors are square at the gum margin, large and creamy yellow. There are 6 cheek teeth on each side of the upper and lower jaw, making 24 cheek teeth in the permanent dentition.

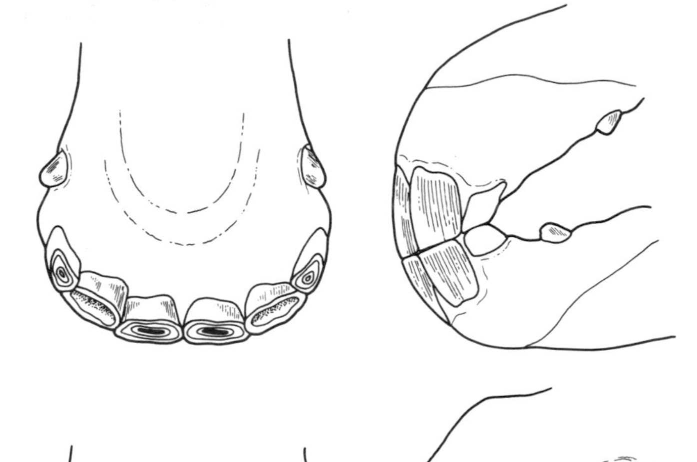

Fig. 55. Dentition of a 4-year-old

Fig. 56. At 5 years of age all the permanent incisors have erupted, and in the male horses tushes are present

When the first 3 permanent cheek teeth erupt they may have the remains (caps) of the temporary premolar teeth stuck on top of them. The cheek teeth are numbered 1 to 6 from the bars to the angle of the jaw. They erupt at 2½ years, 3 years, 4 years, 1 year, 2 years and 3½ years of age.

Male horses and the occasional mare have *canine* teeth (tushes) which erupt, around 4 years of age, in each interdental space. Some horses, especially mares, only have 2 canines instead of 4.

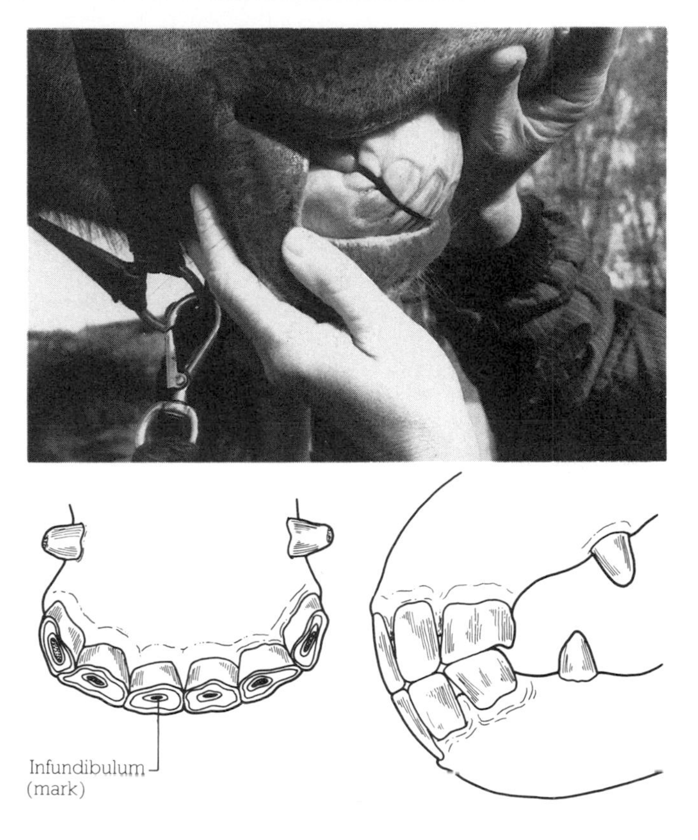

19. A 4-year-old mouth showing permanent central and lateral incisors which are in wear and temporary corner incisors.

Fig. 57. A 7-year-old

Some horses have a very small vestigial tooth (*wolf tooth*) just in front of the upper cheek teeth. These may be present on one or both sides. Occasionally they interfere with the bit and may cause the horse to shake its head. In a few cases they have to be removed, although some wolf teeth are removed to 'treat' the owner, with no benefit to the horse!

Hooks appear on the corner incisor teeth at 7 years and 13 years. Around 10 years of age a discoloured groove (*Galvayne's groove*) appears at the gum margin on the middle of the corner incisor tooth and at 20 years it has reached the biting edge of the tooth.

The incisor teeth are used for tearing and the cheek teeth for grinding food as the jaws move from side to side. These actions gradually wear away the surface of the teeth. The permanent teeth continue to erupt throughout the horse's life. Below the visible crown of the tooth is a reserve crown and below this is the tooth root. About 2 mm (⅛ in) of tooth erupts each year, and as the tooth is 8.5 cm (3½ in) long it takes about 28 years for the whole of the reserve crown to appear.

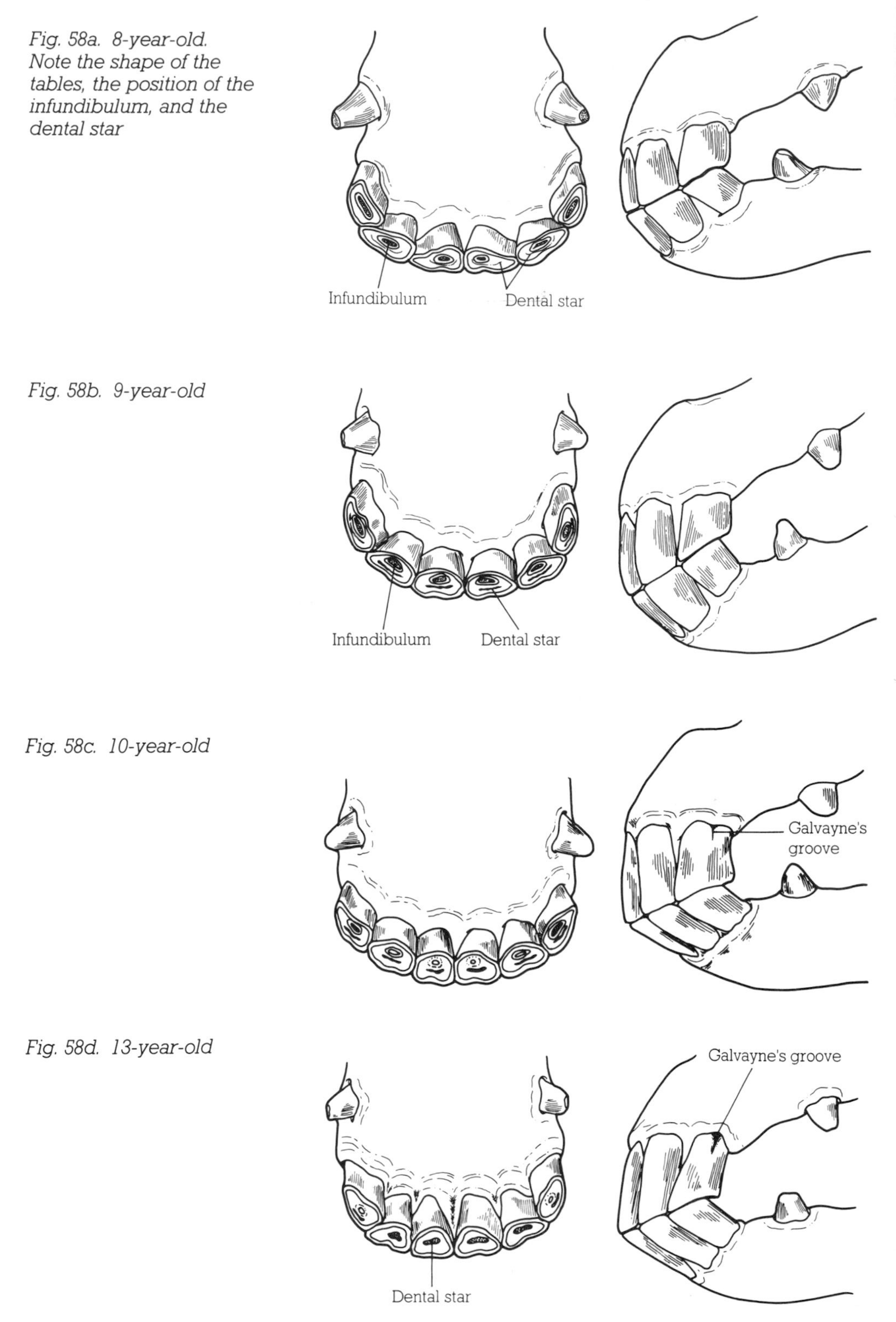

Fig. 58a. 8-year-old. Note the shape of the tables, the position of the infundibulum, and the dental star

Fig. 58b. 9-year-old

Fig. 58c. 10-year-old

Fig. 58d. 13-year-old

The life expectancy of the horse is related to the life span of the teeth.

It is possible to age a horse by examining the incisor teeth. First note the number and type of teeth present, then the angle at which the upper and lower teeth meet, which becomes more acute with age. The shape of the tables, the presence and size of the *mark* (*infundibulum*) and *dental star* (*pulp cavity*), hooks and galvayne's grooves are all used in accurate aging by dentition. Both sides of the mouth are examined.

Dental Problems

Injuries to the jaw, involving unerupted permanent teeth, in young animals may result in abnormally formed teeth erupting at a later date. Horses with teeth deformities, an unusual number or eruption pattern will be difficult to age. Horses with **parrot mouths** (overshot upper jaw) do not have normal wear on the biting surfaces of their teeth. Horses which crib-bite or graze on stoney ground may have abnormal wear on the incisors.

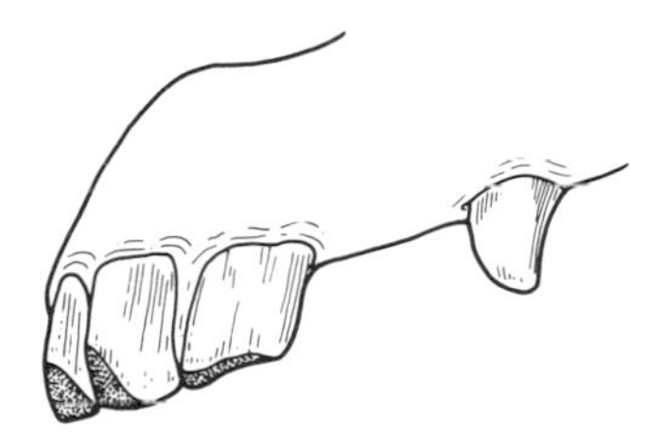

Fig. 59. A crib-biter shows wear on the edge of the upper incisor teeth

If a tooth is lost or removed, the one opposite will become overlong (*step mouth*) and affect chewing. Overlong teeth have to be rasped regularly or cut off with shears.

The mandibular cheek teeth fit slightly behind and inside the maxillary teeth. Because of the anatomy and grinding action of the jaws the outer edges of the upper arcades (cheek teeth) and the inner edges of the lower arcades are not evenly worn, so sharp points develop. Hooks can appear, especially in parrot-mouthed animals, on the front of the first upper cheek tooth and the back of the sixth lower cheek tooth.

Sharp points damage the inside of the cheek and the outer rim of the tongue. Pain from these injuries will alter the grinding movement, so abnormal wear occurs on the molar tables. These abnormalities are described as *wave*, *shear* or *smooth mouths*.

Fig. 60. Points appear on the outer edge of the upper cheek teeth and the inner edge of the lower cheek teeth

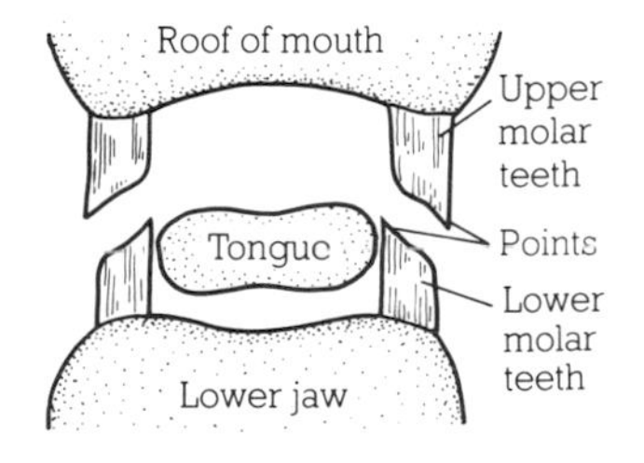

Bit-rings, cheek-pieces and tight nosebands will push the cheeks against points on the upper arcades and result in riding problems.

Infections of the upper cheek teeth and their roots may burst into the *sinuses*, causing a facial swelling and a nasal discharge.

The signs of a dental problem/disease are loss of condition and performance, abnormal chewing action,

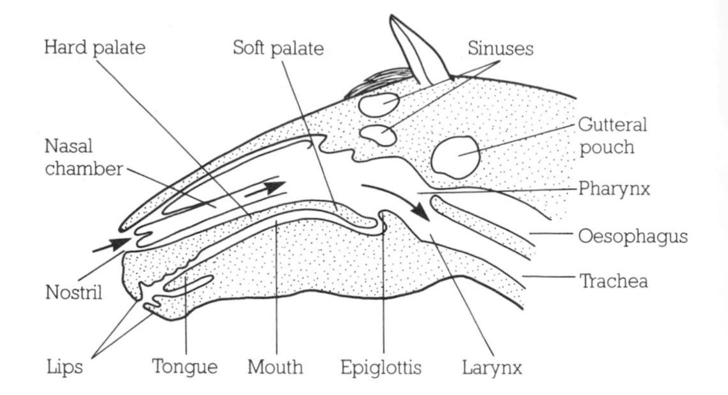

Fig. 61. Position of sinuses

bad breath, nasal discharge, facial swelling and quidding. Salivation, eating slowly and quidding (dropping partially chewed food) are signs of sharp points on the cheek teeth, and the teeth probably need rasping. Painful points can be detected by palpating along the face over the area of the upper arcades.

Examining the Mouth

Some horses object violently to having their mouths examined by striking out with their forelegs and rearing. These animals may be twitched, or chemically restrained with a sedative. If a twitch is being used, the handler should stand to one side of the horse and on no account let go of the twitch in an uncontrolled manner. Twitches make dangerous missiles!

It is best to stand the horse diagonally across the stable with plenty of space in front of it. The headcollar must have a loose noseband to allow the horse's mouth to be opened. Its mouth should not be full of food. A pen-light torch is useful to illuminate the inside of the mouth.

With a quiet, sensible animal, stand at the horse's left shoulder facing the same direction as the horse. Place your right arm under the horse's head with the palm of the right hand on the top of the horse's nose. Then carefully place the left hand into the interdental space, taking care not to catch the tushes. Grasp the tongue firmly and pull it out to the left side of the mouth. The horse will open its mouth, and you can inspect the right-hand side using the torch if necessary. To examine the left side of the mouth, stand on the right side of the horse and bring the tongue out to the right. Do not draw the tongue across the gap between

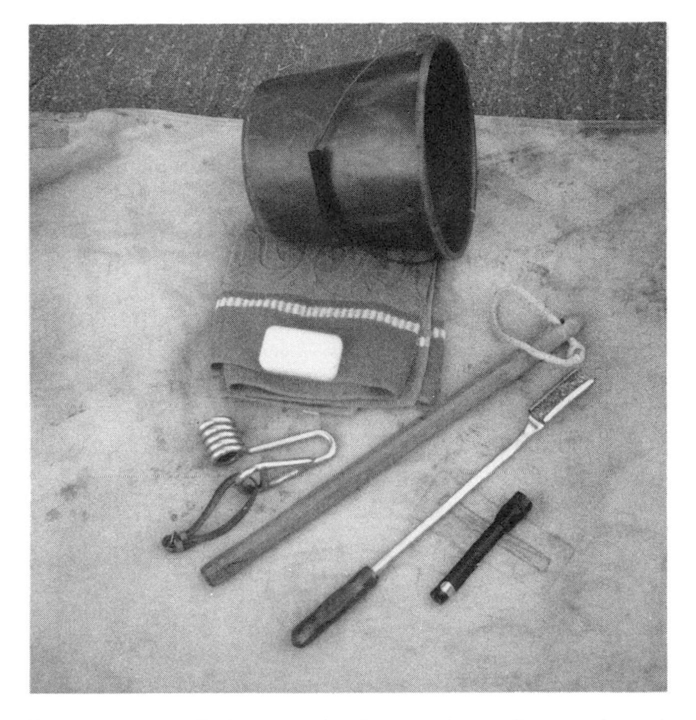

20. A bucket of water, soap and a towel should be provided for the vet. The vet will bring a twitch, torch, gag and tooth rasp, which are all required when rasping and examining the teeth.

the incisor teeth in case the horse closes its mouth and bites its tongue.

Vets can use a metal gag to keep the horse's mouth open. Heavy gags such as the Hausmann's can be dangerous to the vet and the handler if the horse suddenly swings its head about. Some horses object to a gag but do not mind the tongue being held.

Treating Problems

Tooth rasping is a routine procedure, performed by the vet. Tooth rasps come in various shapes and sizes, with angled or straight heads and with different types of blades. They are used for taking off points and small hooks from the cheek teeth.

Overlong teeth and large hooks can be removed with chisels, shears and cutters, and generally the patient would be anaesthetized. The vet will organize X-rays of the head if he suspects diseased roots, sinusitis (infections of the sinus), or abnormal eruption patterns. X-rays are also useful if the length of the reserve crown and root needs to be known.

All horses should have their teeth examined every 6 months. Old horses and those with abnormal dentition may need attention every 3 months.

INTERNAL PARASITES (WORMS)

Virtually all grazing horses and ponies harbour worms in their gastro-intestinal tract (gut). Worms cause various signs of ill health and disease depending on the species and numbers involved, the amount of re-infection from the pasture and the type and frequency of worm control measures practised. A worm-infected animal may show weight loss, a rough staring coat, loss of appetite and performance, abdominal pain (colic), diarrhoea, anaemia, jaundice, swelling and filling of the legs and sheath and in some cases death may follow. Lung worms and round worms also damage the lung tissue and the animal will show signs of respiratory disease e.g. coughing.

Animals which are heavily parasitized are generally debilitated and very prone to other infections and diseases.

The life cycle of the worm varies with the species but it is the adult worms which cause damage to the bowel wall. They shed eggs in the horse's faeces which contaminates the pasture. The eggs hatch out on the grass in the warm and moist conditions especially in the spring and summer to become infective larvae. These larvae are then eaten (ingested) by grazing horses.

Worm larvae may cause damage by migrating through the tissues and various organs of the horse before emerging as young adult worms in the bowel. The time taken for the ingested larvae to reach maturity varies with species as does the migration route.

There are 4 main groups of worms.

1. Strongyles

An important group affecting horses of all ages. It is subdivided into the small and large *Strongyles* (small and large red worms). Horses eat the infective stage-three larvae while grazing.

The larvae of the large red worms migrate through the tissues of the horse, while those of the small red worms (cyathostomes) form cysts in the walls of the caecum and colon for 5 to 18 weeks.

The larvae of *Strongylus vulgaris* damage the wall of the cranial mesenteric artery, the large blood vessel which supplies most of the gut. Small blood clots are dislodged from the damaged wall and cause areas of tissue death (infarcts) in the bowel and episodes of acute colic. The full life cycle takes about seven months. The incidence of *S. vulgaris* infection has decreased due to the widespread use of anthelmintic (worming) programmes.

The cyathostomes have taken their place and cause many more cases of parasitic disease. The main reasons for this are: (1) the cyst wall, which surrounds the larvae while it is in the wall of the caecum, acts as a barrier to the anthelmintic drugs; (2) the small Strongyles have become resistant to most of the Benzimidazole group of wormers.

2. Tapeworm

Anoplocephala perfoliata is the common tapeworm found in the caecum of the horse. The mature tapeworm attaches itself to the gut wall by four large suckers. It sheds segments in the dung which contain large numbers of eggs. The eggs are eaten by forage mites which live in the dense root mat found in permanent pasture land. These mites are eaten by the grazing horse, so completing the life cycle of the tapeworm.

Tapeworms can cause a blockage at the ileocaecal junction (where the small intestine and caecum meet). They may perforate the bowel and cause peritonitis. Horses with tapeworm infestation often show signs of chronic and recurrent abdominal pain (colic).

Tapeworm infection can be successfully treated with pyrantel at double the normal dose rate.

3. Bots

Horse bot flies (*Gastrophilus intestinalis*) lay their eggs on the hairs of the legs, shoulders and abdomen of the horse during the summer months. Larvae hatch out on the hairs and are taken into the horse's mouth when self-grooming. They develop in the horse's stomach and are passed out in the dung the following spring. They have a short pupation stage on the ground before the adult fly emerges to complete the life cycle. The flies annoy the horse when they are egg-laying.

Fly repellents/insecticides applied to the horse's body will stop the flies landing and laying eggs. Any

MAIN INTERNAL PARASITES OF THE HORSE

Type	**Species**	**Site of adult parasite in the horse**
Large strongyles	*Strongylus vulgaris*	Caecum and colon
	Strongylus edentatus	Caecum and colon
Small strongyles	*Cythanostomes* species	Caecum and colon
Roundworms	*Parascaris equorum*	Small intestine
Bots	*Gastrophilus* species	Larva in stomach – adult is a fly
Threadworms	*Strongyloides westeri*	Small intestine
Pin worms	*Oxyuris equi*	Colon/rectum
Lungworms	*Dictyocaulus arnfieldi*	Bronchi
Tapeworms	*Anoplocephala perfoliata*	Ileum/caecum

Drugs Used against Adult Parasites

Anthelmintic drug	Large strongyle	Small strongyle	Round-worm	Pin-worm	Thread-worm	Bot
Piperazine e.g., Crown pony & foal wormer	Poor	√	√	√	X	X
Benzimidazoles e.g., Panacur, Telmin, Equitac	√	√	√	√	at higher dose rates	X
Pyrantel e.g., Strongid P	√	√	√	√	X	X
Ivermectin e.g., Eqvalan	√	√	√	√	√	√

Drug of choice for tapeworm infection is Pyrantel at 2 × the normal dose rate for Strongyles

Drugs of choice for lungworm infections are Ivermectin or Panacur and Telmin at raised dose rates.

small yellow bot fly eggs can be removed from the horse's coat with special bot fly combs or knives or with sellotape.

Ivermectin is the only anthelmintic which will remove the bots from the horse's stomach. Horses should receive this treatment during the winter after the frost has killed all the flies.

4. Lungworm

Although horses and donkeys may be infected with lungworm (*Dictyocaulus arnfieldi*), the donkey rarely shows any signs of respiratory disease but if left untreated may continually reinfect a horse if they share grazing. Infected donkeys will cough up and swallow the eggs produced by the adult worms in the lungs. The eggs hatch out into larvae in the dung and can be detected using a laboratory test. All donkeys are normally treated with ivermectin or a double dose of mebendazole by body weight.

Infected horses develop a parasitic bronchitis and a chronic, persistent cough. The larvae rarely mature to egg-laying adults in the horse so faeces samples are of little use in detecting the infection. Sometimes larvae can be found in samples of fluid taken from the horse's trachea (windpipe). Blood samples will usually show an increase in the number of eosinophils (a type of white blood cell).

Worm Prevention and Control

The veterinary surgeon will advise on a worm control programme which must be tailor-made to each horse. Many factors have to be considered:

i) how many horses and of what age group have access to the pasture
ii) pasture hygiene and management
iii) time of year and climate
iv) which worm species are present
v) presence of drug-resistant worms

The worming programme is normally monitored at regular intervals by taking faeces samples from the horses before and after worming to identify the worm species and check on the worm egg counts. This will show if the drug being used is effective in keeping egg counts low and so reducing pasture contamination. The development of drug resistance can be monitored. (It is well documented that the small Strongyles have developed resistance to most of the benzimidazole group of wormers and are thus immune to them.)

Most worm programmes involve worming at eight-weekly intervals with ivermectin from spring through the summer or every four weeks with other nonlarvicidal drugs to reduce the numbers of small Strongyles on the pasture.

There is normally a seasonal rise in Strongyle egg output during the spring and summer.

From November to February not many eggs will develop into infective larvae because of the low external temperatures.

Horses given a larvicidal wormer, which also kills bots, after the first frosts of winter, will not normally need worming again until the spring.

It is normal to change the anthelmintic drug annually to avoid drug-resistant worms developing. There are three common wormers at present, the benzimidazole group, the pyrantels and the ivermectins. It is important to check the drug name not just the trade name.

Wormers are usually available as pastes, powders, granules or liquids to be given by mouth, either in a dosing syringe, mixed with concentrate feed or by stomach tube.

It is important to dose according to the animal's body weight, using the correct drug at the correct dose rate to remove the species of worms infecting the horse. Treatment will fail if the drug is not correctly administered.

Some wormers remove adult and migrating larvae (larvicidal wormers), e.g. ivermectin.

Any new horses arriving at a premises should be treated with a larvicidal anthelmintic and isolated or stabled for 48 hours before allowing out onto the pasture.

It is normal to worm all horses grazing on the same pasture at the same time, although it has been shown that some individuals have less natural resistance to worms and always have a higher worm egg count than the others.

Pasture Hygiene

Horses are reluctant to graze around dung piles so these areas become overgrown with long rough grass and weeds. If horses are overcrowded on the pasture they are forced to graze the rough areas and will ingest large numbers of infective larvae.

If faeces are removed from the pasture twice a week this will control the level of pasture contamination and increase the area available for grazing.

Small pastures can be cleared manually but large fields are easier to clear if a mechanical sweeper or vacuum is used. These machines do less damage to the pasture than harrows.

Harrowing should only be done in very hot dry weather so that the larvae are killed when the faecal piles are broken up.

If there is adequate new pasture, it is possible to rest certain paddocks to prevent them becoming 'horse-sick' and over-grazed. Paddocks have to be rested for many months so that all the larvae die.

Alternate grazing with sheep and cattle will also remove some of the worm burden from the pasture.

TEMPERATURE, PULSE AND RESPIRATORY RATE (TPR)

It is important for the owner to know their horse's normal body temperature, resting pulse and respiratory rate (TPR) when it is fit and healthy. If the horse is ill, the TPR can then be compared to the normal, healthy values.

Temperature

A large-animal, stout, stubby-bulb thermometer should be included in the first aid kit. The thermometer usually has its own case to prevent breakages, and should be stored in a clean condition in a cool place. Thermometers are washed in *cold* antiseptic solution. Before use, shake the thermometer to send the mercury down to the bulb end, below 35° C (95° F).

Tie up the horse, then stand to the side of the left flank. Hold the tail in the left hand and the thermometer, lubricated with vaseline, in the right hand. Insert the thermometer through the anus into the rectum and hold it against the rectal wall for 1–2 minutes. The reading will not be accurate if the temperature is taken immediately after the horse has defaecated, or if the thermometer is pushed into a faecal ball. The rectal temperature will be raised if taken immediately after exercise or if the horse is excited. Care should be taken not to let go of or break the thermometer while it is in the rectum. Most horses do not object to this procedure as it is not painful or frightening.

As the rectal temperature can alter throughout the day, it is a good idea to take the temperature morning and evening for a few days to obtain an average reading. The normal range for an adult horse is 37–38° C (99–101° F).

If a horse appears unwell, it is usual to take the rectal temperature to see if it is subnormal (below normal) or above normal. If there is any doubt about the accuracy of the reading, the temperature should be retaken. In some viral diseases the fever can be transient and therefore missed unless the temperature is taken frequently. In this case, a normal temperature does not necessarily mean that the horse is not ill.

Pulse

The horse's heart rate increases with fever, pain, excitement, fear and exercise. As the heart muscle contracts and forces the blood into the arteries, the wave can be felt as a pulse. In the horse, the facial artery is commonly used to take the pulse rate. This artery passes over the inside of the bottom jaw bone and is about the width of a pencil in an adult horse. Usually the pulse waves are counted over 30 seconds, timed on a watch, and multiplied by two to give the rate per minute.

No special equipment is needed to take a pulse except a watch with a second hand. It may take a little practice to find the artery and to use the right amount of pressure to feel the pulse wave. It is best to put two or three fingers along the blood vessel, holding it gently against the jaw bone. The horse has a slow resting heart rate compared to humans: 28–40 beats per minute. It is easier to find and take the pulse immediately after exercise, when the rate is faster and the pulse volume is greater. The fitness of the horse can be assessed by the time taken for the heart rate to return to normal after strenuous exercise.

The pulse rate is a good guide to monitor abdominal pain in colic cases.

Respiration

Respiration is the term given to the process by which air is taken into and expelled from the lungs. During inspiration (breathing in) the air enters the nostrils, passes along the nasal chambers to the back of the throat (larynx) into the windpipe (trachea) and then via the *bronchi*, *bronchioles* and *alveolar ducts* to the

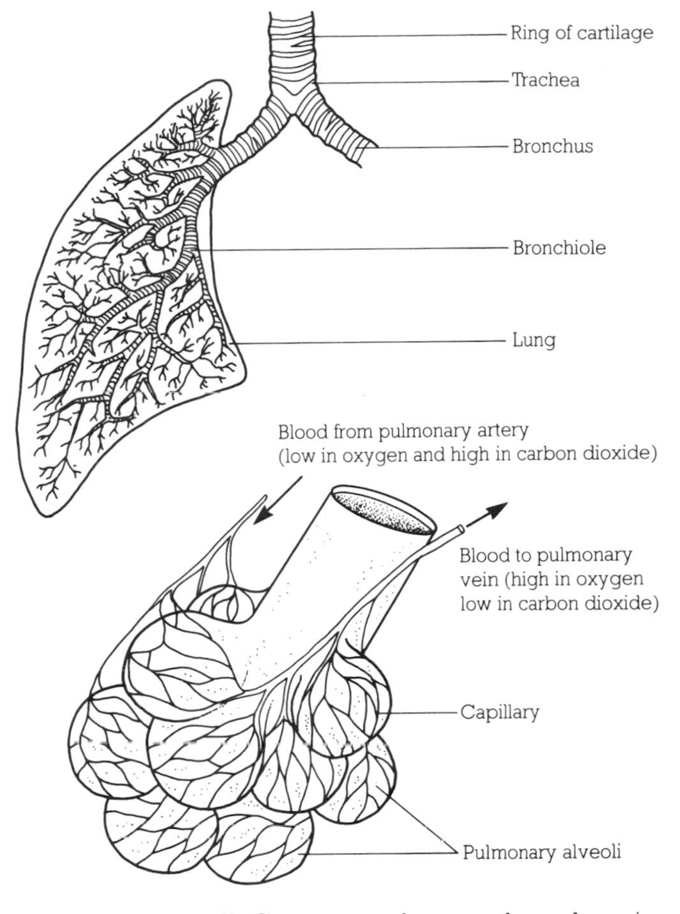

Fig. 62a. The bronchial tree

Fig. 62b.

pulmonary alveoli. Gaseous exchange takes place in the thin-walled alveoli. The oxygen is exchanged for carbon dioxide from the pulmonary capillaries which surround the alveoli. Carbon dioxide is exhaled in the expired air.

The respiratory centre in the brain controls the frequency of breathing by stimulating the intercostal (rib) muscles and diaphragm. The diaphragm is the domed muscular sheet which separates the thorax (chest) from the abdomen.

The respiratory rate per minute in a normal, healthy adult horse is about 12, the normal range being 8–16. The normal ratio of heart rate to respiratory rate is 3:1. The movements of the nostrils or the chest wall can be counted at either inspiration or expiration for one minute to give the respiratory rate. In the normal horse at rest, the movements of the chest wall are slight and shallow, and are best seen by standing to the side of the horse's hindquarters.

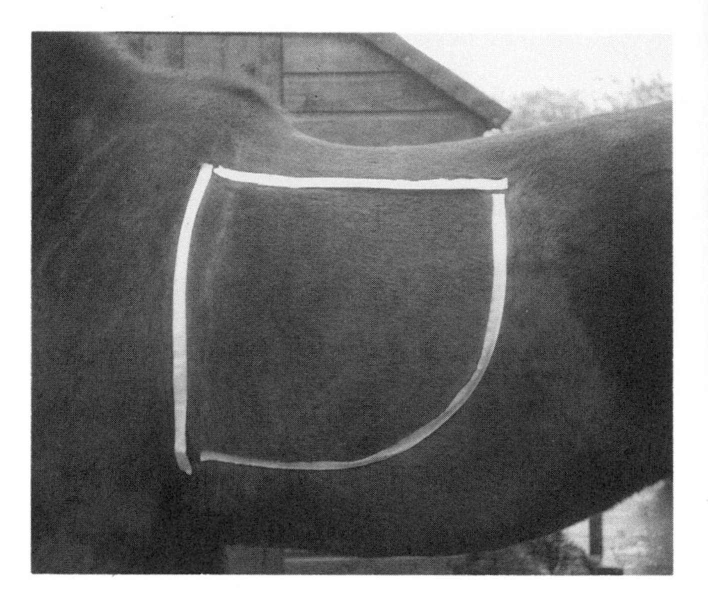

21. Area of chest wall where the vet listens to hear respiratory sounds.

If there is an obvious respiratory effort at the junction of the chest with the abdominal wall, this is usually a sign of respiratory disease. Diseases of the respiratory tract cause an increased respiratory rate.

The horse's TPR should be written in its record book, along with details of vaccination, worming programmes, farrier and veterinary visits, diet and exercise.

If the horse is kept at livery these details must be available to the proprietor of the yard in case they are needed in an emergency.

CHECKLIST –
VITAL SIGNS FOR ADULT 500 KG (1000 LB) HORSE

Temperature	37–38° C	99–101° F
Pulse rate	28–40	per minute
Respiratory rate	8–16	per minute
Daily feed intake	2.5% body weight approx 12.5 kg	per 24 hours 28 lb
Faeces for 24 hours	14–20 kg as 8–10 piles	30–45 lb as 8–10 piles
Fluid intake	20–45 litres	5–10 gallons
Urine output	approx. 5 litres	1 gallon

CHAPTER 10
PREVENTING ACCIDENTS

Many accidents that involve horses and their owners could be prevented with a little forethought and knowledge. Some horses have less sense of self-preservation than others, but also some owners do take the most incredible risks.

The most important rule is to think about what danger the horse could get into, however unlikely, and not to take short cuts or hurry.

STABLE SAFETY

The stable should be a safe place, free from hazards, strongly built and well maintained. It should be of adequate size for the horse to move around, lie down and get up without injuring itself on the walls. The roof or ceiling must be high enough to prevent the horse accidentally hitting its head.

It should be well ventilated but not draughty, and positioned so that it is not too hot in summer or too cold in winter. Wooden stables with metal roofs tend to be like ovens in the summer and are cold in winter. Condensation often drips off the inside of a metal roof onto the horse. Toughened window-glass should be protected by removable grills or bars. Louvred windows are a good design for stables.

The floor surface should be non-slip, durable, impervious to urine, and easy to clean. A slight slope towards the door for drainage is safer than a central drain with a grid. Grids are frequently broken,

22. The bottom stable-door fitted with an anti-chew strip and an animal-proof safety bolt.

allowing the horse's foot to be caught in the drain.

The doorway needs to be wide and high enough to prevent the horse injuring itself on the way through. Horses that have been injured in a doorway tend to rush on through and may knock over the handler. There should be no protruding nails or screw-heads in the woodwork.

Stable doors usually open outwards and are in two halves, the top half being secured open with a hook. The bottom door needs a safety, animal-proof bolt at the top and a kick bolt at the bottom so that the horse cannot let itself out of the stable. Metal anti-chew strips along the top of the door and the frame must be well attached and have no sharp edges. The gap under the bottom door must not be wide enough to trap a horse's foot or leg. Woodwork is often creosoted to prevent the horse chewing it. If paint is used, it should not contain lead or any substance poisonous to the horse.

Horses that kick out at breeze-block walls can fracture their pedal bones (bone in the foot) and develop capped hocks and curbs. Walls can be lined with kicking-boards to prevent these injuries.

Tying-up rings should be situated high up so the horse cannot get its leg caught over the lead-rope and so that when tied up, the horse is in good light and cannot back across the doorway or into the manger. Horses must not be allowed to play with the rope because they can learn to untie themselves. And it is always possible that they will get the rope-clip caught in their mouth or on their lips.

Whichever bedding material is used, it should be of an adequate thickness so that the horse does not develop capped hocks and elbows when lying down. The bed should have wide and high banks to help prevent the horse becoming cast against the walls when it rolls. Horses which roll a lot and frequently get cast should be fitted with anti-cast rollers. The horse must not be left standing on a bare floor for hours as it will be reluctant to stale (pass urine) on to hard ground.

The stable should be well lit with all electric wiring armoured and out of the horse's reach. Safety switches and guards over lightbulbs are essential.

Mangers, water-bowls and hay-racks are common stable fittings. They are made in many designs and materials. Permanent mangers are usually closed in to prevent the horse damaging its knees, and so that it cannot get stuck under the manger when it lies down.

Horses naturally eat at ground level, but some animals insist on knocking over feed containers and water buckets, becoming entangled in metal handles, etc. There are a number of indestructible feed-bowls and water-buckets that cannot be broken and will not cause injuries to the horse should it stand on them. Water-buckets can always be placed inside a rubber tyre to prevent them being knocked over. They can also be attached to the wall by a variety of brackets and hooks.

Automatic water-bowls are an alternative to buckets. They should be easy to switch off in case of leaks, and regularly checked to make sure they are working. The main disadvantages to these bowls is cost, and the fact that the water intake of the horse cannot be easily monitored.

Hay may be fed in racks, nets, or off the floor. Off the floor is wasteful, and the hay may become

23. An electric safety switch and a screw-on guard over a power point.

contaminated with faeces and urine, but the horse's head and neck posture is that of a grazing animal – natural. It is easier to weigh the hay in a net and there is less waste. Animals which paw the ground may easily get a leg caught in a low hay-net and suffer rope burns and other injuries. It is important to hang a hay-net correctly, with a quick release knot, and at a height at which the animal is unlikely to catch its leg (even when the net is empty and therefore lower).

Horses are unlikely to become caught in a hay-rack, but they are eating with their heads and neck held high and may get hay seeds and dust in their eyes.

No mucking out tools or other equipment must be left in the stable with the horse, there is no point in inviting trouble! It is important to be tidy around the stable and work in a methodical manner. Once a good routine is established there is less danger of accidents and mistakes.

Naturally no one should smoke anywhere near the stable yard, and the fire drill and position of the extinguishers and fire buckets should be known by all the personnel on the yard.

TURNING OUT SAFELY

The stable should have a good wide access so that the horse does not have to turn sharply through the doorway. Narrow passages leading to stables should be avoided.

However close the turnout paddock or field is to the stable-yard, the horse should never be allowed to charge out of the stable into the field on its own. It must be led on a headcollar and rope, and walk out in a controlled manner, turn around to face the gate and stand quietly while the headcollar is removed. This good-mannered behaviour is part of the basic training of the horse.

Horses which are allowed to career out of the stable may slip or fall onto the yard, become impaled on the gate-post or gate-catch, or knock over the handler. It also encourages the horse to barge at the door as soon as it opens.

It is best not to leave the horse's headcollar on it when it is out at grass as they have a habit of becoming hooked onto fencing, etc., and can then damage the horse's head.

SAFETY IN THE FIELD

Numerous accidents happen to horses out at grass, and commonly involve other horses, bad fencing, and ponds or ditches. Wasteland, old tips and land over lead mines are not suitable places to graze horses, neither are gardens.

Kick wounds are the commonest injuries horses inflict on each other, although bite wounds are sometimes seen. It is important not to put too many animals on a small area. If there is plenty of grass and plenty of space – 2 acres per horse – there will be less kicking. If the group is constantly changing there will be a lot more injuries. It is best not to put a strange horse into an established group of horses but to introduce newcomers to one horse at a time.

Often fields are split into mares or geldings in order to prevent fighting. It is unwise to put foals and young horses in with larger shod animals.

Kicking and fighting often occur at feeding times. If only one animal is to be fed it should be removed from the field. If hay is being fed, the piles should be well spread out. There should be twice as many piles of hay as there are horses so that the fast eaters will not bully the slow eaters.

Horses that are known to kick and fight are best grazed on their own. If a group of horses are galloping around together one may get kicked accidentally or forced into a fence. A horse which has not been at grass for some time is best exercised before turning out and kept without food for a couple of hours, in the hope that it will graze quietly rather than gallop about.

24. Gate-bolts can become impaled in the horse as it goes through the gateway so this type of gate-bolt is not suitable for use near livestock.

25. Hedge, stone wall and post-and-rail fencing.

Many horses are put out in fields with protective boots on their legs. Boots must not be too tight, nor must they come loose and rub the limbs. New Zealand rugs are commonly used on horses in the winter, especially if they have been clipped. Rugs are only safe if they are secured with a roller/surcingle, breast and leg straps. Horses can become entangled in rugs that are hanging off.

All paddocks need safe, stout fencing and well-hung gates. Gate-catches which protrude beyond the gate can become impaled in the horse. Gates leading onto roads should be padlocked.

Hedges and stone walls make good, safe boundary fences and afford shelter for the horse. Post-and-rail fencing is common for horse paddocks but must be well maintained. Broken rails can cause nasty injuries

26. Barbed-wire injuries are extremely common in horses and often caused by wire which is loose or broken.

that contain wood splinters. Plain wire, if pulled taut, is preferable to sheep-netting or barbed wire. Horses tend to get their feet caught in sheep- or pig-netting, damaging the bulbs of their heels or pasterns.

Barbed wire injuries are extremely common in horses, and especially foals. Barbed wire should be avoided if at all possible. Electric fences can be successfully used in pony paddocks. You can hang coloured pieces of plastic from the wire to make it more visible, so the horses do not accidentally run into the wire. Newer types of fencing made from plastic and rubber are safer than wire or rails. Although initially expensive, they may work out cheaper if accidents are prevented.

Gaps in fences should be properly repaired, and not filled with makeshift pieces of rotten wood, pieces of metal or corrugated sheets.

Table 2 – Poisonous plants

Plant	Symptoms of poisoning
Acorns Bryony Buttercup	abdominal pain (colic) diarrhoea
Bracken Horse Tails	central nervous system (CNS) affected CNS inco-ordination, ataxia weakness, emaciation, anaemia
Hemlock Laburnum Nightshade	colic, diarrhoea, CNS signs
St Johns Wort	photosensitivity of the skin
Ragwort	CNS signs – circling & head pressing, weight loss, diarrhoea
Privet Laurel	colic, ataxia
Ground Ivy	rapid breathing, increased temperature, weak pulse, conjunctival haemorrhages
Foxglove	tetanic spasms, loud heart
Yew	muscle haemorrhages, excitable followed by collapse
Wild Arum	abortion (if pregnant!) inflamed mucous membranes of the mouth and eyes

Fields by roads often have the extra hazard of people throwing rubbish into them. Any rubbish should be removed from the field – including garden refuse and grass cuttings. All poisonous plants, e.g., ragwort, yew, laurel, bracken, privet and shrubs must be removed from the pasture (see Table 2). Oak trees can be fenced off to prevent the horses eating acorns in the autumn. Fruit trees may also be a problem if they have an abundant crop. The fruit should be gathered to prevent the horse gorging itself.

Horses at grass will still need a constant supply of fresh water. Automatic-filling water troughs are convenient, but must be thoughtfully positioned in the field so that the horses do not get trapped between the trough and the fence. A stream or pond may be the source of drinking water, but they must not be used if they become stagnant or contaminated. Horses may become trapped in the mud as the water supply dries up in the summer or caught in the ice in the winter.

Old baths with taps do not make suitable water troughs. Many horses end up with fractured jaws when their head-collars become caught on the taps.

Horses should not be allowed to graze near greenhouses, farm machinery, swimming-pools, mine shafts or septic tanks. Many septic tanks and mine shafts have rotten wooden lids that a horse can easily fall through, and it is extremely difficult to lift them out.

Foals and very old animals can easily get stuck in ditches and die of exhaustion. These types of hazards should be fenced off to keep livestock away from danger.

Field Shelters

If the field has no hedges or trees, it may be necessary to provide a three-sided field shelter to protect the horse from bad weather in winter and flies in summer. The shelter must be large enough to accommodate all the horses in a field. The walls of the shelter must reach the ground – any gaps are dangerous as limbs may be trapped under the walls. Old farm buildings in bad repair do not make suitable shelters as horses may be injured by falling masonry and roof timbers.

Care must be taken when tying up a horse in a field in case it pulls away still attached to a rail or gate. Horses panic if they are dragging gates or rails behind them and may break a leg.

ROAD SAFETY

Riding on the roads is always potentially dangerous as many motorists have no knowledge of horses, and travel too close and too fast when overtaking them. Even on the quietest bomb-proof horse, accidents can happen, and traffic accidents involving horses frequently end in the destruction of the horse. Only competent riders should go on public highways. They must be aware of the Highway Code and the BHS road safety rules.

The horse should be well shod with road nails to prevent it slipping on the tarmac, and knee-boots and normal brushing or exercise boots should be worn. It is important that you are clearly visible to the other road users – fluorescent tabards, exercise sheets, armbands and legbands are easily seen. It is extremely dangerous to be riding at dusk or in the dark, even with stirrup lights.

Nervous, young and excitable animals are best kept off the road. It is dangerous to canter along grass verges at the side of busy roads in case the horse stumbles on the uneven ground, or shies at something in the hedge. Also, rubbish such as tin cans and glass is frequently dumped on the verge. It is obscured by the long grass, and may frighten or trip the horse.

Continual trotting on roads or any hard surface will cause excessive wear and tear on the horse's limbs due to jarring and continual concussion, and this causes traumatic arthritis to the lower limb joints (fetlock and pastern).

The rider must maintain a rein contact, send the horse forward and be attentive at all times without being tense and alarming the horse. Take care when passing parked vehicles, gateways and pedestrians, all of which can cause the horse to shy out into the road. If the horse is nervous do not stand it at the side of metal railings or cattle grids in case it jumps into them when large vehicles pass by.

Some normally quiet roads may become busy at certain times of the day, so it is best to avoid riding along these roads at those times.

TRAVELLING SAFELY

The horse-box or trailer should be in a road-worthy

condition. It is vital that the ramp and the floor are in good order. It is very common for a horse's foot to go through rotten floorboards, resulting in a serious injury.

More accidents occur when loading and unloading the horse than in transit. The box should be positioned on level ground and away from any hazards before loading/unloading the horse. The horse may step off the side of the ramp and get its leg trapped against a wall or fence or another vehicle.

The horse will need protective clothing for travelling. It is irresponsible to travel a horse wearing only a tail bandage and no protective boots on its legs. Bandages and boots only afford protection if they remain in place so make sure that they are put on correctly. Overreach boots are used to protect the heels, knee and hock boots are also essential, as is a rug with surcingle or roller, and some type of poll-guard to protect the top of the horse's head.

Never be in a hurry when loading the horse. Always leave plenty of time, make the inside of the box light and as inviting as possible, and give the horse a reward when it loads.

If the journey is long, the horse will need water at regular intervals. It is very tiring to travel standing up, especially when balancing as the vehicle goes around corners and stops and starts. On arrival at its destination the horse should be allowed to walk around and relax, and be given adequate time to rest before further exercise or journeys.

Horses will normally travel well and load easily if they have a good journey, and this means a thoughtful driver!

Most trailers and horse-boxes have tying up rings on the outside, although this is not an ideal place to tie a horse as there are many protruding bolts and pieces of metal on the exterior of the box which could injure the horse. It is also not uncommon for horses to be loose on the showground after becoming untied from the side of a vehicle.

At a competition it is safer to leave the horse tied up with a hay-net inside the vehicle, but even then the horse should not be left unattended for any length of time. Vehicles must be parked in the shade in hot weather. It is not safe to travel a horse untied or without a partition in the trailer, as they have been known to jump out of the back while in transit!

SECTION 4
COPING WITH ILLNESS AND INJURIES

CHAPTER 11
ASSISTING THE VET

HORSE RESTRAINT

Horses are large and extremely strong and must be treated with respect. It is important that they are correctly handled at all times as they are capable of causing serious injuries to themselves and their handlers. It is easy to be over-confident and careless when dealing with a familiar animal, and even a good-mannered, well-trained horse may react unpredictably when in pain or frightened.

All horses should be taught to tie up on a headcollar and rope and to stand still. They should be capable of being lead on a headcollar and bridle at walk and trot.

Good-quality tack in good repair is unlikely to break when the horse is handled. It is sensible to wear gloves when leading a horse. Never wrap a rope around your hand. When handling fractious horses it is advisable to wear a skull cap and shoes which will protect your feet if stepped on. Always stand in a safe place; close to the shoulder is a good position to avoid being bitten, struck by a front leg, stepped on or kicked. Some horses have a nasty habit of leaning on people and crushing them against walls. When handling the hind legs, stand as close to the flank as possible to avoid the full force of a kick.

Small children should *never* be allowed unsupervised near a horse, and *never* be asked to hold an animal for the vet or farrier. They can easily be accidentally injured. Loose dogs are also a hazard around horses and cause accidents.

Holding the Horse

Horses may have to be held while receiving veterinary attention. They may be held on a headcollar if indoors or on a bridle if outside. The handler should stand on the same side of the horse as the vet. If it reacts badly it can then be pushed away from both people. The handler must be alert and pay attention to the horse's reactions, not be engrossed in watching the vet!

It is unnerving for the person examining the horse if they have no confidence in the handler! If the horse is in strange surroundings or having an unusual procedure such as a X-ray examination, it is sensible to restrain it on a bridle.

Sometimes an animal which reacts violently to injections in the neck muscle will tolerate an injection in the brisket or the hindquarters. Horses which are difficult in the stable are often quite well behaved out of doors and vice versa. It is important to inform both the vet and the farrier if the horse is known to behave badly for a certain procedure. Owners are often afraid to admit to the vet and farrier that their horse is difficult, in case they refuse to see it, but there is nothing more annoying than being kicked and then to be informed that the horse reacted that way last time! Forewarned is certainly forearmed with these horses. If a problem can be anticipated it is easier to deal with and to avoid injury.

Manual Restraint

Some procedures require that the horse stands still for a few minutes, and it may be necessary to divert its attention by using various forms of manual restraint.

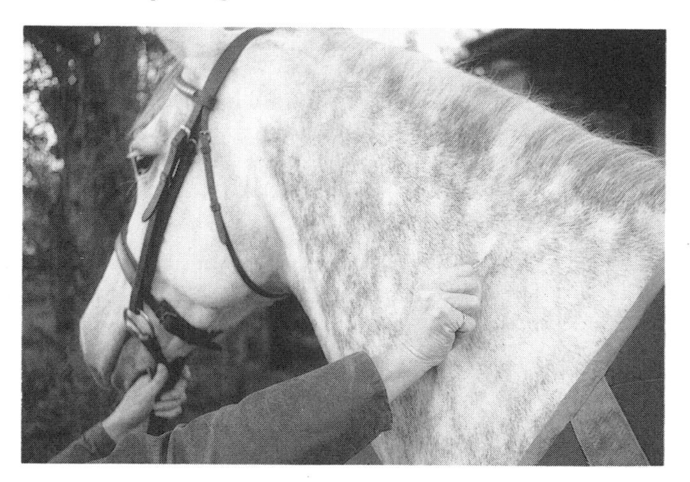

27. Grasping a handful of skin as a means of restraint.

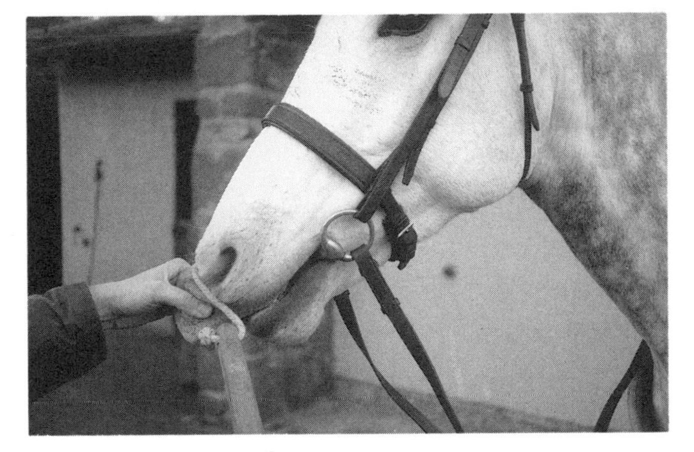

28. Applying a twitch.

The horse's ear may be held quite firmly but not twisted (as this can damage the cartilage) in one hand, while the headcollar rope is held in the other hand. A handful of skin on the lower third of the neck or a roll of skin on the shoulder can be grasped firmly to make the horse stand quietly. Alternatively, the end of the nose can be twitched with a hand, taking care not to block the nostrils. This is a most useful, quick method of restraint.

Twitches can be made from various lengths of wood with a soft rope loop threaded through a drill hole in the end. Nylon baler-twine loops can cut into the nose if twisted tightly. Metal, nutcracker-type twitches are available from veterinary wholesalers and large saddlery shops. They are quicker to apply than a rope loop, which has to be twisted onto the nose. However, if the horse struggles, the skin on the nose may be pushed into the hinge and cut. Twitches with extra-long wooden handles have to be held with two hands. The handler can usually avoid the front legs of the horse as they are at a safe distance. The only problem is finding someone strong and capable enough to keep hold of the twitch.

Twitched horses are usually calm and relaxed. Twitches act in a similar way to acupuncture by causing the release of chemicals called endorphines, which have a soporific effect on the horse.

If a horse is known to be awkward or dangerous for a particular procedure, it is best to apply the twitch at the beginning of the procedure while the horse is calm. It can be difficult to apply a twitch on a horse that has become highly excited or fractious. If the horse is adequately restrained from the start, the examination can be carried out calmly, quickly and safely without unduly alarming the animal.

A few horses cannot be twitched as they become extremely angry and quite dangerous. In these cases it is safer to use a sedative.

It is often easier to apply a dressing to a front leg if the other front leg is held up. If a hind leg is being treated, the front leg on the same side should be held up. Some agile animals can manage to kick with a hind leg while the front leg is held up, and balance on the other two legs!

Some horses behave well if blindfolded or if a hand is cupped over the eye so that they cannot see the examiner. This method is handy when measuring a horse that will not allow the measuring stick near it. Some horses which are difficult to inject will stand perfectly still provided they cannot see the syringe.

Chemical Restraint

Horses may need to be chemically restrained using a *sedative* or *tranquillizer*. All horses should have a heart and lung check prior to using these drugs.

Sedatives depress the activity of the brain and are used to calm a nervous, excitable or vicious animal. By reducing the animal's awareness and alertness, they make pain more endurable. They also cause drowsiness. Tranquillizers cause sedation without drowsiness. Some sedatives also have analgesic (pain-killing) properties.

Sedatives can lower blood pressure and body temperature and depress respiration. Some drugs also cause paralysis of the muscle which retracts the penis into the sheath, so must be used with care on geldings. These drugs should not be used on breeding stallions.

Horses are usually dosed by body-weight, but the effect achieved does vary from horse to horse depending on its temperament and the presence of external stimuli, such as noise.

There is usually a maximum calming effect at a certain dose rate. By increasing the dose a greater effect is not achieved, and unwanted side effects such as inco-ordination may result. For the desired result these drugs should be administered to a calm animal, that is, before it has become alarmed or excited. This is possible for procedures, such as shoeing and clipping, which are arranged in advance. Some drugs will make the animal sweat so are not suitable to use for clipping.

A sedated animal may become unsteady on its feet, so

care must be taken if a leg has to be held up, as in shoeing. Sedated animals should not normally be transported in case they fall over in transit.

The sedative may last for at least 20 minutes to an hour or so depending on the drug, the dose, the health and temperament of the horse.

It is unwise to use a twitch on a sedated animal as it may fall over.

FIRST AID CARE FOR WOUNDS

Accidental wounds are very common. They may be trivial, like a scratch, scrape or abrasion, where a small amount of hair and the uppermost layer of the epidermis is partially removed. Abrasions show pinpoint bleeding, and although initially painful they are usually quick to heal. They should be cleaned and protected from further injury and contamination.

Skin wounds are classified according to their size, shape and involvement with deeper structures.

Puncture wounds involve a small entry hole which may heal trapping infection, tissue debris and foreign material in the tract below. The puncture track may travel deep into the underlying tissue where the airless environment is ideal for the multiplication of anaerobic bacteria such as *Clostridium tetani* (see page 90).

Useful First Aid Kit and Medicine Cupboard Contents

Thermometer
Vaseline
Twitch
Torch
Watch with second hand
Bowl (stainless steel)
Plastic measuring jug
Scissors
Large dosing syringe
Surgical gloves
Soap
Kitchen roll or towel
Polythene bags
Note pad & pen
Thermos flask
Hoof knife

Dressing materials:
- gauze swabs
- cotton wool/gamgee
- kaltostat/melonin
- bandages/tubigrip
- animalintex
- barrier boot
- pressage stocking

Antiseptic wash e.g. Hibiscrub/Pevidine
Eye wash
Hexocil shampoo
Anthelmintics
Friars balsam or Menthol or Oil of Eucalyptus

Zinc and castor oil ointment
Insect repellent
Lasonil
Antibiotic ointment or powder or spray (ask vet to supply)

First Aid Equipment for Wounds

Stainless steel bowl
Plastic measuring jug
Large plastic dosing syringe to irrigate wound
Pair of curved scissors
Thermos to carry ice or hot water
Twitch
Antiseptic to clean hands e.g. Hibiscrub or Pevidine
Pair of surgical gloves
Mild antiseptic to clean wound e.g., sterile normal saline or Milton diluted with boiled water
Gauze swabs or cotton wool
Non-adhesive dressing e.g. Melonin or Kaltostat
Cotton wool/gamgee/disposable nappies
Bandages or tubigrip or pressage stocking
Paper towels or kitchen roll
Polythene bags
Foot dressings also require a barrier boot or similar protective boot

Bruises involve bleeding under the skin. The amount of swelling is related to the size of the damaged blood vessel. The haemorrhage can be controlled by applying cold-packs and pressure. If commercial ice-packs or cold bandages are not available, a pack of frozen peas or a polythene bag of crushed ice applied over a wad of gamgee or a folded towel are just as effective.

Lacerated wounds are large with jagged skin edges exposing the underlying tissue, which is frequently damaged and torn. There may be considerable muscle damage with pockets where debris and fluid collect. These wounds are usually grossly contaminated and bleed profusely. There may be areas of skin loss or tags of skin and muscle which will die due to a loss of blood supply.

Wounds with full-thickness, straight-skin edges are **incised wounds**. These wounds, if fresh, can normally be sutured (*stitched*). This holds the skin edges closely together to promote rapid *first intention healing* (the name given to the process whereby the

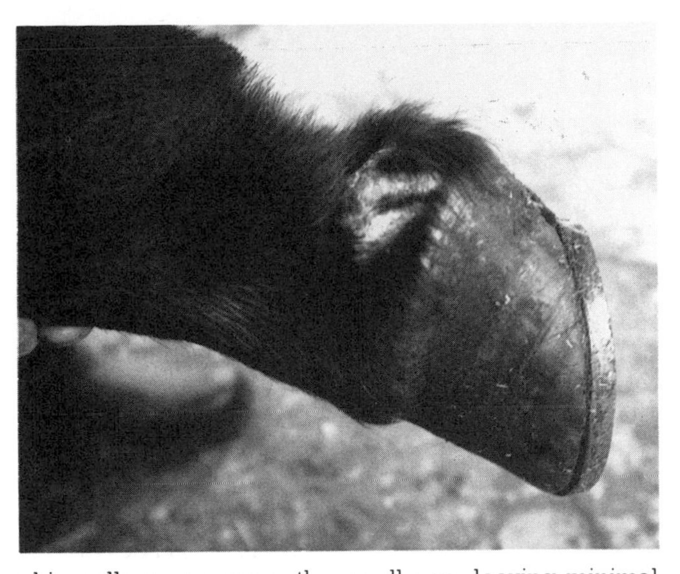

29. Scar tissue on the heel after the wound has healed by second intention.

skin cells grow across the small gap, leaving minimal scar tissue). Wounds over 2.5 cm (1 in) long involving a full thickness skin are normally sutured. Wounds over joints are difficult to suture and often burst open when the joint moves. Plaster casts or firm bandaging are usually applied to prevent movement disturbing the sutures.

Wounds involving joints, tendons, tendon sheath and eyes are all serious, and require urgent veterinary attention.

Stopping Bleeding

Wounds may bleed profusely. It is worthwhile remembering that a horse has about 38 litres (10 gal) of blood and a small volume of spilled blood does appear to go a long way. Bleeding occurs as a steady flow from veins or in spurts from an artery. Haemorrhage must be controlled before any other first aid treatment is attempted, and the application of firm pressure will stop most bleeding. Hold a wad of gamgee firmly over the bleeding vessel and if possible bandage it into place until veterinary help arrives. If the blood oozes through the first layer of dressing add another layer on top, and if need be a third layer. If first aid equipment is not available, use any article of clothing or material in an emergency. Don't worry about sterile dressings as the wound will already be contaminated and infected, and this can be controlled at a later date with antibiotics.

The horse should be kept calm and still as any movements will tend to dislodge the clot. All unwanted spectators, other horses and other animals should be kept away from the injured horse. The horse may need to be rugged up. In summer time a fly-sheet should be used.

Wounds to the lower limb – knee, hock and below – are normally bandaged to prevent further tissue damage and contamination, to control swelling, stop haemorrhage and to keep the skin edges close together. Wounds on the body and neck can be kept clean and free of flies by covering with a clean, cotton sheet or large towel (roller towel).

Wounds may be contaminated with grit, gravel, sand or soil. Large lacerated wounds can have foreign material such as fragments of glass or splinters of wood in their depths. Puncture tracks may contain wood or metal. It is vital when cleaning a wound not to drive this surface rubbish further into the tissues, and a large dosing syringe is much preferred to a hose-pipe. The tissues should not be repeatedly waterlogged.

Treating the Wound

Before treating the wound, assess the size and depth, what structures are likely to be involved, the amount of haemorrhage and tissue loss, and the presence of foreign bodies. First aid should cause no further damage to the tissues.

All the equipment, dressing materials, hot water, etc., should be prepared before the horse is restrained. Surgical gloves can be worn if the hands cannot be adequately cleaned. There is no point in carefully cleaning a wound with dirty hands that have just picked out the horse's feet!

If the haemorrhage is not great then the wound can be treated as follows. Firstly the hair around the wound should be removed, using scissors or hand-clippers, taking care not to drop the hair into the wound.

Wounds should be cleaned with a mild antiseptic solution, which will not irritate the tissues. Commercially available plastic packs of sterile normal saline can be used, or boiled water, or a weak solution of Milton. Sometimes warm solutions are better tolerated by the horse. Gauze swabs or pieces of cotton wool soaked in the solution of choice (as recommended by the vet) are then carefully used to clean the wound. This should be done in such a way that the clean area is not contaminated by dirty solution trickling onto it.

Once the area is clean and free from all obvious foreign material, a non-adhesive dressing is applied. Melonin or Kaltostat are preferable to paraffin gauze if the wound is to be sutured as grease is difficult to remove from the wound.

If the wound is on a limb, the dressing can be held in place by cotton wool, gamgee, disposable nappy or tubigrip under a slightly elasticated, conforming bandage such as Vet Rap.

If the wound requires veterinary attention, do not use sprays, ointments or powders before the vet has examined it. It is impossible for the vet to examine a wound adequately that has been plastered in purple spray, black powder or green ointment. Ask your vet for advice on wound treatment and aftercare.

Open wounds not suitable for suturing heal by *second intention*. Granulation tissue fills the tissue deficit and as the wound contracts, this brings the skin edges closer together. Delicate epithelial cells grow across the granulation tissue and so suppress the formation of excess tissue. Sometimes the granulation tissue continues to grow above the level of the skin which is trying to cover it. This exuberant granulation tissue is called proud flesh and is common on lower limb injuries in the horse. In this site, wound contraction plays an insignificant role in wound healing so the epithelium has a greater area to cover. The epithelial cells prefer a moist environment, free from bacteria and irritating substances such as rough dressing materials or bedding, and free from constant movement, in order to multiply. Sometimes cell fatigue occurs and the new border of epithelial cells stop multiplying, this allows the proud flesh to mushroom out over the skin edges. Proud flesh should be removed surgically to just below the surrounding level of the skin. Pinch grafts can then be placed into the granulating bed to form islands of skin which will grow out to meet each other and so cover the wound. The skin at the edge of the wound is sometimes surgically treated to encourage the cells to start multiplying.

Horses which have not been recently vaccinated with tetanus toxoid will require a tetanus antitoxin injection if they are wounded, however trivial the wound may appear. Some wounds are so grossly contaminated and infected that the horse requires a course of antibiotics. If there is considerable swelling and pain, the vet will also prescribe analgesics.

Looking After an Injured Horse

Large wounds may require daily cleaning by swabbing with a weak solution of antiseptic. Ask your vet which one he recommends.

Various ointments are used on or around wounds. Fly repellents or insecticidal solutions can be used around the wound or ointment such as Acriflavin is safe to place on the wound surface. Antibiotic creams, ointments, solution and powders are also useful on open wounds to control surface infections. Large wounds which exude large amounts of serum are associated with scalding and chapping of the skin below the wound. This area can be protected with vaseline or zinc and castor oil ointment.

Where the skin is intact, bruises can be encouraged to disperse by using an appropriate ointment e.g. Lasonil applied to the skin surface.

Most horses with extensive limb injuries will require stable rest and possibly walking out in hand. If the horse is very lame it is best to put it on a shavings or paper bed as straw tends to wrap around the injured leg. Shavings irritate tissue so the wound should be well protected with dressings.

Horses with wounds must be on a good ration with adequate protein, Vitamin A and zinc. The vet treating the case will advise on aftercare, exercise and diet. It is best to write down any instructions given by the vet and make sure that you understand the details of any medication, dose rates, etc.

Bandages and Dressings for the Legs

With the availability and popularity of exercise and travelling boots, the art of bandaging has been lost through lack of practice.

Bandages are routinely used to keep wound dressings in place and to support injured tissue, to control swelling and haemorrhage and prevent excessive movement of the joints. Woollen stable bandages are useful to keep the limbs of old and sick animals warm. Bandages should be snug and firm with equal tension over their entire length. Incorrectly applied bandages with inadequate or lumpy padding may cause pressure sores and skin sloughs (dead skin falling off). Young animals are especially susceptible to skin necrosis (skin death) from pressure rubs.

When using bandages it is important to cover a decent length of the leg, not just the small area which may be injured. If there is a wound or swelling on the lower limb, the bandage should cover the area from the coronary band to the knee or hock. If the knee or hock are involved these should be bandaged separately so that the hock or knee bandage is overlapped by the lower limb bandage.

Wet, dirty or contaminated bandages should be replaced by clean dressings. Extensive wounds to the forearm or thigh may result in swelling of the lower limb. This may be prevented by firmly bandaging the lower limb using plenty of gamgee as padding to control the swelling.

The traditional white open-wove cotton bandage which is non-stretch, non-adhesive, and non-conforming is difficult to apply neatly to a horse's leg. As it does not stick to itself (cohesive) it requires tape to fasten it in place.

There are many new types of bandage that are suitable for use on horses. The easiest to apply are those which do not stick to hair or skin, but do adhere to themselves so preventing the layers from slipping, and require no fasteners. Bandages are now made of light, soft but strong material that will support and conform to the area being bandaged. Slightly elasticated bandages give more support than non-stretch bandages and only allow limited movement. Good bandages should not fray, and should be resistant to wetting. The most useful size for the limbs of adult horses are 10 cm (4 in) wide by 5 metres (16½ ft) long. Smaller ponies may require 7.5 cm (3 in) wide and 4 metres (13 ft) long.

Most veterinary practices will supply their own clients with suitable bandages, otherwise chemists and saddlery shops often sell horse bandages.

Elastoplast is a useful adhesive bandage to cover other bandages where more immobility and support is required. Elastoplast is fairly resistant to wetting and is hard for the horse to remove by chewing. Pepper, curry powder and crib box can be applied to bandages to deter the horse from removing them. If all else fails a neck cradle or a muzzle can be used on the horse.

If elastoplast is used, care must be taken that it does not stick to the horse's hair or skin. Horses object to elastoplast being removed if it is attached to the coat. This will often make an otherwise quiet horse react violently to having dressings changed. For this reason elastoplast is not popular as a dressing material for horses.

Cotton wool or gamgee tissue are commonly used as padding under a bandage. Cotton wool frays and is easy for the horse to pull out from under the bandage. Wool fibres easily stick to wounds and are difficult to remove without soaking them off.

Folded towels and disposable nappies can be used under bandages. Nappies are a very good fit on horses' feet!

There are various types of sterile non-adhesive dressings which can be applied directly onto wounds. Melonin consists of a perforated film surface over an absorbent pad which draws the exudate away from the wound. Kaltostat is an ion-active absorbent wound dressing with calcium alginate in the fibres. The calcium ions in the dressing react with blood and exudate to form a gel layer over the wound surface, which provides a good moist environment for effective healing. It is easy to remove and can be used on drier wounds providing it is soaked in saline (salt water) first.

Soft, paraffin-impregnated tulle or gauze dressings are also non-adherent, sterile and individually wrapped for ease of use. They may also be impregnated with antibiotics to treat infections on the wound surface.

Lycra stockings are available in various sizes to fit the knee, hock and fetlock, they are zip-fastened with velcro at the top and bottom to conceal the zip. They are used to hold dressings in place, and being elasticated give some support and pressure to the limb. If the hock or knee stocking are used it is advisable to put a padded bandage over the stocking from the upper cannon bone to the coronary band. This will prevent any swelling appearing on the lower limb below the stocking.

The hock and knee stockings are the most popular as these areas are difficult to bandage successfully. It is easy to cause pressure sores on the boney areas such as the point of the hock and accessory carpal bone. Tubigrip can also be used in these sites. As it is an elasticated tubular stocking it has to be pulled over the hoof. This is much easier in practice if a polythene bag is first placed on to the foot. This will also keep the tubigrip clean. It should be pulled up above the area it is being applied to and then pulled downwards so that the hair lies flat. This forms a snug, supporting 'bandage' which moulds to the contours of the leg. For greater support tubigrip can be applied as double thickness.

It is awkward to keep foot dressings dry and clean and in place. When there was an abundance of hessian sacks the corners were useful to tie over a foot dressing. The alternative is to use one of the commercially available plastic or rubber boots. The lightweight, vinyl plastic *barrier boot* is made in 5 sizes to fit small ponies up to large horses. It is about as difficult to pull on as an overreach boot and is unlikely to fall off.

Barrier boots keep the whole foot clean and dry. The *shoof* is very easy to put on, but as it does not completely enclose the entire foot, it is apt to swivel around and fall off accidentally. The heavy rubber *equiboot* fastens with wire and the inside of the boot has a number of metal studs which may press into the coronary band if the foot has not been adequately bandaged beforehand.

Poultices such as animalintex are easier to use than kaolin and are less messy. Hot poultices are used to soften the hard dry horn of the sole prior to paring it, in cases of infection. The poultice is trimmed to size and applied over the area to be softened not over the entire sole. A piece of gamgee or a disposable nappy is used to hold the poultice in place. This is covered in a conforming, cohesive bandage and a barrier boot.

Owners tend to be over-keen on using poultices. It is not a good idea to apply them to a skin surface for many hours. They waterlog and chap the skin, which allows bacteria on the skin surface to penetrate the deeper tissues. Over-zealous use of poultices cause infected, hot, swollen and painful legs. The vet then has to treat the original condition and the one created by the owner!

Badly injured limbs, such as lower limb fractures or injuries to joints or tendons, may require splinting so that the horse can be moved safely. Splints prevent movement of the limb and so prevent further damage.

The leg should be dressed as normal with enough padding to stop the temporary splint from injuring the tissues. A piece of plastic gutter cut to size with the ends well padded makes an ideal splint. In order to immobilize the injured area it is necessary to include the joint above and the joint below the injury in the splint. The splint can be attached to the padded leg using elastoplast. If plastic guttering is not available pieces of wood can be used e.g., broom handles.

Hoof repair materials include epoxy resins, plastic packing and acrylics. These are hard and prone to cracking and cannot be nailed into. Artificial horn repair material e.g. Supa is textured so that it can be trimmed, rasped and nailed into like actual horn. These materials are used to repair defects in the hoof wall, preventing dirt working its way into the deeper sensitive structures of the wall.

Horses which cannot be shod with a conventional metal shoe can be fitted with glue-on, plastic shoes. These are very useful for horses with thin or broken walls or horses that cannot tolerate the farrier nailing on a metal shoe. These plastic shoes are used by vets and farriers in treating horses with laminitis and other foot diseases.

VETERINARY/CLIENT RELATIONSHIP

Horse owners normally register with a veterinary practice as soon as they take ownership of an animal. This is the right time to enquire about routine visits for vaccination, worming and dental care.

The practice will let owners know what time to telephone to arrange non-urgent or routine visits and what the procedure is for out-of-hours emergencies. Out of hours normally means evenings and weekends. There may be a set time each day when the vet is

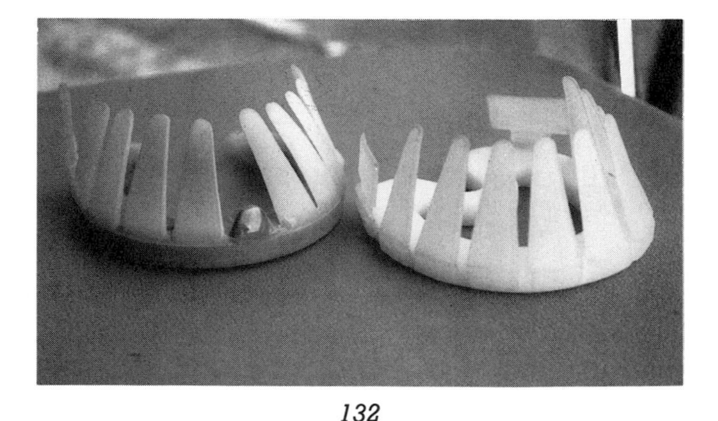

30. Two designs of glue-on shoes. Used on animals with broken hoof walls which cannot have nail-on shoes fitted.

available to give advice on the phone. All veterinary practices provide a 24-hour cover every day of the year. This service should not be abused. No one appreciates non-urgent enquiries late at night, week-ends or at meal times. Vets like to eat and sleep like other normal human beings!

CHECKLIST – EMERGENCIES

Emergencies that require urgent veterinary attention include:

fractures
profuse haemorrhage
colic
respiratory distress
collapse
acute laminitis
eye injuries
penetrating wounds to the chest, abdomen, joints and tendons
difficulty in foaling

- A vet should be contacted immediately and given an accurate description of the location of the horse and the nature of the emergency. The name and address of the owner must be supplied, with the telephone number, where the practice can return the call if necessary. It is therefore advisable to keep the telephone free.
- Ask how long it will take the vet to arrive at the scene and what first aid measures should be used in the meantime.
- Sometimes more than one practice is contacted for veterinary assistance and in this case the owner must be prepared to pay for all veterinary visits.
- While waiting for veterinary help, the horse must be kept calm, quiet and warm.
- If an accident occurs in a public place, all bystanders should be kept as far away as possible.
- In a road traffic accident, the horse and the handler must be protected from further injury from oncoming traffic. It is worth mentioning that not all policemen have knowledge of horses, nor are they always

competent at handling them. Flashing lights and sirens are not conducive to keeping the horse calm! It is best to ask the police to control the traffic flow and keep the public away.

- To save time when the vet arrives, arrangements should be made for transport and stabling, so that everything is ready for the horse once it has been treated. If a bridle or rugs are needed someone should be sent for these. If the emergency occurs at night, arrangements should be made to provide adequate light either by torches or car headlights.
- Horses with leg injuries find it easier to walk up a trailer ramp than the steep ramp of a horse box. Sometimes they are more willing to walk backwards especially if a foreleg is injured.
- If the horse is seriously ill, or has sustained injuries that will require a general anaesthetic in order that it can be adequately treated, the insurance company should be informed. Most companies have an answer telephone service, so messages can be left out of normal office hours.

A routine visit provides an ideal opportunity for the vet to get to know the horse, the owner and the premises where the horse is kept. This is helpful should the vet then be called out at night to an emergency, because the vet will already know the locality of the stables, what facilities are available, and the temperament of the horse. It is also an advantage to know how the horse reacted to routine health procedures.

When arranging a visit make sure the receptionist is aware whether the condition is urgent or not. Give good directions so that the vet can find the horse. A detailed accurate history of the problem is important. Do not leave out information which may mislead the vet. Most vets prefer the owner not to use home remedies on the horse prior to the consultation. It is always best to seek professional advice early on in an illness.

When booking a veterinary visit, always let the practice know how many animals the vet is coming to treat, then adequate time can be allowed for the visit. The vet will then be punctual for the next visit on the list. Do not ask the vet to look at extra cases or problems on arrival or just as he/she is about to leave the yard.

No vet specializes in every condition which may befall a horse, but they will know where to find a second opinion and make referrals to specific experts should this be necessary.

The owner must have the horse ready to be examined when the vet arrives, it should not still be out in a field miles away! If possible the horse should be clean and dry, and if the feet are to be examined they should be picked out but not covered in hoof oil. Any equipment such as headcollars, tack, boots, etc., which may be needed should be already at hand.

An adult must be present to handle the horse and discuss the treatment and progress of the case. A child cannot give permission for veterinary procedures, they cannot sign consent forms, nor can they be expected to take care of medicines. Even though the horse or pony may belong to a child, the parents are legally responsible for it and should always be present at veterinary visits.

It is always appreciated if water, soap and a towel are provided for the vet when the examination has finished. Any instructions should be written down so no mistakes are made.

There is no point in asking and paying for professional advice and then not taking it. If the vet advises complete box rest this means keeping the horse in the stable at all times. It does not mean walking the horse about on the yard or grazing it in the field. If advice is not followed it is unlikely that the animal will make the expected recovery. Vets usually find out when owners have not followed instructions and this leads to problems in the vet/client relationship.

Most insurance companies ask to be informed by the owner of an insured animal as soon as it becomes ill or requires veterinary attention. Usually claim forms for veterinary treatment are provided by the insurance company. The owner is liable for any fees incurred and should seek reimbursement from the insurance company. The insurance company does not usually pay for forms to be completed by the vet, the owner is responsible for these fees.

When owners are arranging holidays, it is best to inform the vet when they will be away and who will be looking after the horse, just in case they need to call the vet out.

If the horse requires veterinary attention while at a show, it is important to write down any details of treatment to give to the horse's usual vet on returning home. Always inform the show duty vet if the animal has any allergies or has been on any medication before it receives treatment.

ADMINISTERING MEDICINES

Vets often leave medicines for the owner to administer to the horse. The dose, frequency and method of giving the drug should be written down in order to avoid mistakes. The instructions should be followed carefully. Only drugs which have been prescribed by the vet should be used on the horse. Never use a drug prescribed for one animal on another animal and never substitute one drug for another. Always check that it is the correct drug, the correct dose and the correct patient.

Do not use inadequately labelled drugs, or drugs which have passed their expiry date, or drugs which have been incorrectly stored and have changed their appearance.

All medicines should be stored in a locked, cool, dry cupboard. The medicine cupboard should contain a diary for keeping a detailed record of all medicines used. Unsupervised children should not be allowed to administer medicines to horses.

Medicines must not be mixed into feeds that are left in a feed-room to be fed at a later date. This practice leads to mistakes where the wrong horse is given the medicated feed, with serious consequences.

Medicines are either given by mouth, by injection, by inhalation or locally. Powders, pills, pastes and liquids are usually given orally (by mouth). They are commonly mixed with a small amount of a concentrate feed or sometimes added to the drinking water.

Pastes are usually dispensed in a dosing syringe and put directly into the horse's mouth. The horse is restrained in the same way as for examining its mouth. The mouth must be empty of all food material so when the paste is squirted onto the back of the tongue it will be swallowed. Some horses are quite adept at spitting out paste when it has not been placed far enough back in the mouth or has stuck onto food material.

If pills or powders are added to a feed, it is vital that

the horse eats the entire feed and does not waste any medicine by dropping it into the bedding, over the door or onto the floor. The horse should be watched while it eats the medicated feed. Some horses are reluctant to eat doctored feeds. Fussy eaters can be encouraged to eat by adding treacle, honey or apple juice to the feed to disguise the medicine.

Medicines should not be added to feeds if the horse has a poor appetite as this may stop it eating altogether. It is wiser to mix the powder or pills into a paste with treacle or honey and dose it orally using a dosing syringe. Alternatively the mixture can be spread on bread and given as a sandwich! Small pills can easily be pressed into the flesh of an apple or ripe pear and then offered to the horse.

The owner should inform the vet if the horse has not received the medicine for whatever reason. The drug may then be given another way, such as by injection.

Medicines which have to be dosed in large volumes or have an unpleasant taste are usually given by stomach tube. The vet passes a rubber or plastic tube into the nostril through to the pharynx where it is swallowed going down the oesophagus into the stomach. This method allows the correct dose of a drug to be given at the correct time.

Drugs may be injected subcutaneously (under the skin), intramuscularly (into the muscle), or intravenously (into the vein), using a sterile syringe and needle. The diameter and length of the needle will depend on the site of injection. The size of the syringe depends on the volume of the drug being used. Most drugs are dosed according to the animal's body weight. Most vaccines are given by deep intramuscular injection as are the majority of antibiotics.

Drugs which should be administered by intramuscular injection may cause a severe reaction if accidentally injected into the blood stream. Drugs which are meant to be given intravenously may cause pain, swelling and muscle damage if injected into a muscle or into the tissue surrounding the vein.

Some drugs, such as those to treat allergic respiratory disease, are given as a fine spray through a specially designed face-mask.

Menthol, oil of eucalyptus and friars balsam can all be added to boiling water to give a vapour which, when inhaled, helps loosen nasal and upper respiratory tract discharges. Care must be taken to avoid scalding the horse's muzzle while it inhales the steamy vapours. Usually a small amount of hay is placed in a bucket with a few drops of the inhalant and about 2.5 cm (1 in) of hot water. The horse's muzzle is held over the top of the bucket.

Locally used drugs include skin preparations, eye ointments and drops. It may be necessary to clip away the hair prior to using an ointment on the skin, as when treating mud fever (see page 59).

Care must be taken when using any eye preparation not to damage the surface of the eye with the nozzle of the tube or bottle. The nozzle should be held parallel to the eyeball not pointing at 90° to the eye. If the hand holding the medication is rested against the horse's head there is less chance of stabbing the horse in the eye should it suddenly move. Eye lotions are used to clean away dirt and discharges, they should be sterile and isotonic (same concentration) with the tears. The horse will tolerate preparations on the eye surface if they are slightly warm.

NURSING THE SICK AND INJURED HORSE

The importance of good nursing cannot be over-emphasized. The vet can diagnose an illness and prescribe medications, but frequently the nursing makes all the difference between recovery or not, especially in diseases where the animal's own defence system and the body's healing process play a major role in recovery.

Sick animals must be provided with shelter from extremes of climate and temperature. A roomy, quiet box, which is well ventilated and is at a constant temperature, is ideal. In some conditions, such as tetanus, absolute quiet is essential.

The bedding material should be thick, warm, dry, comfortable and dust free. The banks must be big enough to prevent the horse from getting cast. Animals that are ill should not wear themselves out struggling to get up.

Horses with respiratory diseases are normally bedded on shavings or paper. When possible the stable should be mucked out while the horse is outside, so that it does not inhale any dust or ammonia fumes from the urine. In bad weather the horse cannot be turned out of the stable, nor should infectious animals be moved from stable to stable.

Horses with colic tend to dig up the bed, so it is left in heaps, with holes down to the concrete. The bed has to be frequently tidied up so that the horse does not injure itself. Straw beds may be eaten in between bouts of colic, so the horse has to be muzzled or put onto a shavings bed.

Straw is not a suitable bedding material for very lame horses as it tends to become wrapped around the legs.

In winter, lightweight warm rugs and woollen stable bandages should be used. If the horse is feverish and sweating a woollen blanket or thermatex rug should be placed under the other rugs to prevent the horse from becoming chilled. Rugs must be removed and shaken twice a day to remove bedding material and to check for pressure sores or rubs on the horse.

In the summer, the stable must be kept free of insects which would annoy the horse. It may be necessary to use a summer or fly sheet.

The horse should be groomed regularly without tiring it. The eyes, nose and dock must be sponged. Any discharges can be wiped away using damp cotton wool. The nostrils can be smeared with vaseline to make the removal of discharges easy and prevent the muzzle from becoming sore. All contaminated material should be bagged and burnt.

Special care must be taken when nursing infectious animals to prevent transmitting the disease to other horses. The stable should be isolated from the rest of the yard by roping it off and keeping unnecessary personnel away. Protective waterproof clothing which can be easily disinfected should be worn by the 'nurse'. A bucket of disinfectant should be provided to wash all boots when leaving the stable. All utensils used in the stable must be kept away from the rest of the yard.

A hospital-type chart can be kept by the 'nurse' to record TPR (see page 140), daily intake of food and water, amount of urine and faeces passed and medications given. The treatment, prognosis and nursing should be discussed with the vet together with any problems encountered. The vet will advise on the amount of rest and exercise the horse should have.

Most sick horses do need to rest so it is important that the 'nurse' isn't constantly in the stable. The horse should be allowed to rest between grooming and administering medicines or changing dressings or rugs.

Record Chart for Sick Horses

	Date		Date	
	AM	PM	AM	PM
Temperature				
Pulse rate				
Respiratory rate				
Feed				
Water				
Faeces				
Urine				
Medications				
Comments				

Stabled horses will need their feet picking out and inspected twice a day to prevent thrush. Very lame horses may develop laminitis in feet which are bearing extra weight. The vet will advise on frog supports for the feet which are at risk.

Bandages must be frequently checked for rubs, contamination, unpleasant discharges and any increase in pain from the area bandaged. Horses must be prevented from chewing wounds and dressings. Pepper or mustard or curry powder can be put onto bandages to prevent the horse chewing them. Neck cradles are sometimes used to prevent the horse removing dressings.

Horses which have sustained large wounds will need a good plane of nutrition. Sick animals often have a poor appetite so it is important to feed best-quality and easily digestible rations. Often warm feeds stimulate the appetite. Carrots, apples, pears, treacle and alfalfa make a ration more appetizing. Frequent, small feeds should be offered to the horse so that it is not over-faced. Any feed which is not eaten should be removed from the stable, not left in the feed manger.

Injured animals may be reluctant to move, as will those in pain, so the feed must be in a position where the horse can easily reach it. Sometimes animals are thought not to be hungry when in fact they cannot reach the food. Horses with stiff necks will need to be fed and watered off raised buckets. Hand feeding may be necessary to encourage the horse to eat.

Horses with thick nasal discharges should be fed at ground level to help drainage. It is often advisable to steam the head with oil of eucalyptus or menthol prior to feeding. This may encourage the horse to eat as it will improve its sense of smell.

Fresh, clean, cool water must be available at all times. Even if the water has not been touched and looks clean it should still be changed three or four times a day. Automatic water-bowls are not suitable for sick animals as it is important to monitor the water intake.

HORSES IN OLD AGE

Aged horses (over 18 years) require frequent dental care, every 3–6 months, as dental problems become more common with old age. They may have difficulty in grazing because of dental disease or loss of teeth, or due to arthritic conditions. Special diets are often needed to keep old horses in good bodily condition. They may find it difficult to eat roughage, so grass nuts or grass meal or complete nuts can be used. They may require vitamin supplements: vitamin B1 to withstand stress; vitamin E for muscles; folic acid to stimulate blood cell production, vitamin A for healthy skin and eyes and vitamin C to help fight infections.

They may need extra grooming as self-grooming is often difficult due to stiffness. Old horses that are arthritic are reluctant to lie down and roll because they have difficulty in standing up again.

Skin tumours are common on older horses. These may ulcerate and attract flies and become infected. Fast-growing tumours should be surgically removed before they reach an unmanageable size.

Old horses need regular, light exercise to prevent muscle wastage and stiffness. Abnormal wear on the shoes is often the first sign of gait alteration due to joint pain and stiffness. To improve the quality of life, low doses of analgesics (painkillers) will make light exercise and grazing less stressful for the horse.

Old horses tend to stand about in the field and should not be grazed with young, boisterous animals that are likely to kick.

It is extremely important that shelter and warmth is provided in the winter time. Warm, lightweight rugs and wool stable bandages will help the horse through the winter. In summer time they will need protection from flies and shade from strong sunlight.

When a horse has finished its athletic career it should not be retired out onto a field and forgotten about. It should receive just as much care and attention as when it was young.

Many old horses die quietly in their stable or field, but unfortunately sometimes the owner has to make the sad and distressing decision to put the horse down (euthanasia). Owners often ask their veterinary surgeon's advice but the ultimate decision is the owners'. If the horse is in constant pain and miserable and not enjoying a normal life the owner usually makes the brave decision. Most vets will destroy the horse in its home surroundings so that it is not distressed by travelling to an abattoir. Horses are either destroyed by injection of an overdose of anaesthetic, or shot humanely.

INDEX

Page numbers in *italic* refer to the illustrations